Zeropolis

TOPOGRAPHICS

Zeropolis
The Experience of Las Vegas

Bruce Bégout

Translated by
LIZ HERON

REAKTION BOOKS

To Vincent Puechegud

Published by Reaktion Books Ltd
79 Farringdon Road, London EC1M 3JU

www.reaktionbooks.co.uk

First published in French as *Zéropolis* © Editions Allia, Paris, 2002

English-language translation © Liz Heron 2003

Photographs by Julie Cook

This work has been published with the support of the Centre National du Livre, French Ministry of Culture

The publication of this book is supported by the Cultural Service of the French Embassy in London

Liberté • Égalité • Fraternité
RÉPUBLIQUE FRANÇAISE

Printed in China

British Library Cataloguing in Publication Data

Begout, Bruce
    Zeropolis: the experience of Las Vegas. - (Topographics)
    1. Las Vegas (Nev.) - Description of travel
    2. Las Vegas (Nev.) - Social life and customs - 20th century
    1. Title
    979.3'135

ISBN 1 86189 176 8

Las Vegas never was more than
the largest lightbulb in the world.

J. G. Ballard
Hello America

Contents

Preface

I myself am the Babylon
from which I must flee.
John Donne

Anyone planning to write about Las Vegas runs a serious risk of
looking like the wet blanket who, in the midst of the festivities,
cuts short the laughter and the dancing to make a speech that is
bound to sound tediously in contrast with the party mood.
However, by way of immediately pre-empting any such attri-
bution of sorely misplaced context, I could plead that it has not
been my general intention to celebrate the architectural and
social event represented by Las Vegas, nor to trace its geneal-
ogy. I have not even sought to elevate my prose to the over-
weening heights of its ambient phantasmagoria. So what is the
purpose of this book? Or rather: what is it I wished to retain of
this urban experience?

It strikes me that I would not be very far from the truth if I
were to answer anyone who happened to ask me what I had
learned in Las Vegas with the perfectly simple reply: 'Nothing.'
I would mean by this not only that the town itself resembles
nothing, pure urban chaos, but I would also be saying that I saw
nothing there that I didn't already know. Which is to say that in
a way Las Vegas represents nothing more than what is all
around me these days as an ordinary *homo urbanus*. This observation might seem strange, not to say mistaken. Isn't the world
capital of gambling viewed by everyone as an expression of
pure fantasy and boundless eccentricity the like of which is to
be found nowhere else on earth? To be more accurate, isn't it a

town that provokes worldwide astonishment or sarcasm on account of its passion for excess?

To tell the truth, I think that whatever new objection is raised, I shall stand my ground and say that Las Vegas is nothing more than our everyday cityscape. What has become established in the middle of the Mojave Desert: the might of entertainment dictating the flow of life; the organization of the city through shopping malls and amusement parks; non-stop, day and night bustle in the streets and covered walkways; themed architecture that combines commercial seduction with childlike make-believe; the subjugation of city dwellers by an opium of televisual spectacle (since the casino hotels of Las Vegas correspond to TV shows represented in three-dimensional form) – are all things we are already familiar with, and will be induced to become even more accustomed to. No matter where we live: Paris, Cape Town, Tokyo, São Paulo or Moscow, the culture of consumerism and recreation that has transfigured Las Vegas for nearly thirty years daily gains more ground in our everyday relation to the city. We are all inhabitants of Las Vegas, however far away we are from southern Nevada. Its name is no longer a fantasy. It lives in our heads, is expressed in our ordinary gestures.

This is the reason why our urban environment is already shaped by the main distinguishing features of Las Vegas, whose pseudo-edifices of fantasy contain the formula for our lives to come. Thus each trip we take to a shopping centre is a shadow cast by Las Vegas habits and customs. That Las Vegas is only the final destination awaiting us is equally confirmed by the fervour with which every city in the world sets out to renovate its old industrial areas with the implantation of leisure complexes and shopping malls that barely conceal their inspiration. Of course, and this must be acknowledged as an inherent property, the city of gambling makes *everything bigger*. It wants to be huge and boundless. In Nevada the most tenuous of our everyday experiences is expressed in enlarged and amplified form. But this is just a shift in scale, not in nature. Whatever one might think of the waves of tourists that inundate the city all year long, the mercantile and infantile logic that directs the city with a hand of iron is not so much extra-ordinary, as hyper-ordinary. It takes our most commonplace actions and paints them on a bigger canvas: playing, eating, consuming, having fun.

These were my first feelings, on the basis of a stay in Las Vegas in the mid-'90s. Over time, they have grown, have become more defined and have given rise to this sequence of short texts, like so many urban tableaux grabbed from the city out of the window of a moving car. I would not be completely honest about my intentions, however, if I did not amend what I have just said in some small measure. In Las Vegas I saw something quite out of the ordinary. In a way such as I had never before experienced, with gleeful savagery the town takes apart the whole cultural, social and aesthetic caboodle which usually surrounds our actions and gestures. Whether it is a matter of institutions (weddings, christenings etc.) or traditions, Las Vegas makes fun of everything. It makes every reality an object of mockery. Without any concern for history, it pulps all human events into an electrochemical swill of parody which leaves absolutely nothing in one piece. In so doing, it uncovers the primeval scene of society: the impossibility of believing in the truth of the other. It turns others into perfect strangers, since all the culture and civilization that signals their presence is thoroughly ridiculed here. For the first time excess turns into lack, and the capital of exaggeration lets incidences of total deficiency show through: cultural, social and aesthetic poverty. Under its haemorrhage of light and spectacle of every kind, it shows up a cruel yet necessary truth which has to be faced if we wish to go on living: 'it is all just a huge and grotesque farce'.

But if, in certain respects, the urban decor of Las Vegas is equivalent to some gigantic modern *vanitas*, it equally shows us that what happens there nevertheless has little to do with our erstwhile carnivals, when the *memento mori* of masks and costumes still possessed some critical function. Whereas the annual festival allowed the inversion of roles and the transgression of rules, for its part the urban amusement park that is Las Vegas only reproduces, if not underlines, social and economic segregations. The antisocial violence of the city, its lawless, creedless nature, which could have led to an unusual political posture, as the first an-archist city in history, is in fact carried out for the sake of a goal which is unfailingly and wholly traditional and conservative: *for certain people to profit thereby*. There too the alleged folly of Las Vegas confirms our reality more than it alters or corrects it. Thus, everything that has governed the desire to write about this non-city finds its source in the seminal intuition that what is afoot there reveals nothing less than the direction taken of late by our market culture, which is probably working its final sleight of hand: the Utopia of leisure and non-stop fun. The reason I have chosen Las Vegas to highlight these disturbing instances of our new urban experience, is that it is their birthplace and I am convinced that the shadows by themselves give emphasis to the depths and throw outlines into relief.

Zeropolis

Like a fragment of a still incandescent comet that has just smashed into the ground, Las Vegas shines in the distance of the Mojave Desert night.[1] With its thousands of fitful garish glimmerings, it illuminates the celestial vault, which puts on a pallid show by comparison. One might imagine it as a giant funfair fallen from outer space which, casting its final glow into the sky, reaches out to find its natural home. But this vision is only a dream and first appearances are deceptive. The bright light that blinds us as we near it does not issue from the stars, it merely comes from the hydroelectric power station on the site of the Hoover Dam which, day in day out, supplies the city with millions of kilowatt-hours.

The first images offered by the city increase this violent impression of explosiveness. Like the lightning that combines heat and electricity, Las Vegas literally detonates. Through the car window, you breathe in the heavy and oppressive exhalations of an approaching storm. Once you are in the gloomy outskirts, the first flashes can be seen a long way off. As you head into the town on Interstate 15, the unreal colours of the illuminated signs begin to snake across the sky in every direction. But you don't feel at all worried by it. The danger is elsewhere.

Now while you drive *up and down* (in the full meaning of the words) the centre of town, you remember that it was in this immediate vicinity, on vast military bases hidden deep in the desert, that innumerable atomic tests took place, earning Nevada the unenviable designation of the Nuclear State. Yet the Bomb was not always something to be feared. In the 1950s the casinos exploited the geographical proximity of the nuclear tests and made them an emblem of the town. There were *atomic* parties, *atomic* hairdos, *atomic* cocktails. Ignorant of the risks of nuclear radiation (the Federal government only made them officially known at the start of the 1960s), some hoteliers even organized picnics to the north of the city so that people could get a *live* view of the spectacle of the terrible mushroom cloud exploding. In 1953, in its brochures, the Atomic View Motel gave its own guarantee of an unimpeded view of the *phenomenon* from any of its rooms.

Nowadays the dangers of nuclear radiation are better known, and this tragic phase in the history of the town seems to wish a veil to be drawn over it (besides, most of the onlookers aren't there any more to give their own versions). All the same, the secondary effects of the Bomb can still widely be felt. Almost everything in the town's most habitual way of being brings to mind a conflagration: the demographic *explosion*, the economic *boom*, the *mushrooming* city, etc. Las Vegas was born to radiate, to flash, to explode. A nuclear city, though one without a core, where everything, from parking spots to motel rooms, from casinos to shopping centres, becomes fission and eruption, where the most modern technology vies for space with the oldest: gambling. A mirthful and all-devouring abyss of energy, the capital of gambling has thereby set itself under the double seal of electricity and atom, wave and shock.

Caught inside this energy maelstrom of watts and hertz, you can't so much as touch a door handle or a metal object without at once receiving, by way of welcome, a little electric shock which gives you an unpleasant start. Electricity is everywhere in cables and in human flesh, wrapping itself around the slightest thing. It has become substance and properties, subject and qualities, embodied in matter, air and water, running quickened over every single surface. Like the tunic of Nessus, it sticks to the skin. Under its unalloyed sway, every body becomes an immense electrical conductor, whose task is to store the ambient energy produced by the countless signs, spotlights and integrated circuits. Recharged like a battery, one then rushes in a state of trance to the fruit machines to empty out this overload of electrical power that threatens to make us likewise implode.

Outside (though does outside really have any meaning here where interior and exterior, covered and open are muddled into one continuous, almost mental space?), regulated like clock-work, thousands of neon tubes curved every which way endlessly wink, to the point where they totally blind any onlooker foolish enough not to have made sure of just looking at them sideways. For the space of a night, they give life to the red and mauve spray of the Rio, the Riviera's cascade of sparkling diamonds, the brightly dripping ice cream cone at the Glitter Gulch. In this insubstantial night where everything is streaming out around itself, the incandescent lights and the indistinct sounds, the fabulous sums displayed in gold letters on never-ending lines that run straight down through the streets, the glittering advertisements that crack like luminescent whips over bruised retinas, MUCH MORE BUCKS, and the giant $$$$$$$ that ripple out at the rate of an oceanic flow, there is no possible vanishing point for the eye.

HIGH HIT FREQUENCY SLOTS – BONUS FLUSH
ACES & JACKS – VIDEO POKER – ROYAL MANIA

WE PAY YOU TO PLAY $$$$$$$$$$$$$$$$ WE PAY
YOU TO PLAY

Each of these sights seems to drop back onto the same single plane, where it can be distinguished only in its outlines, thereby flashing up with even greater brilliance. Contrast holds sway, to the point of the total splitting off of every shape into precise, sharp-edged figures; a kind of hyper-perception which blots out the blurry fringes of the gaze, the imprecise edges of the visual field, those halos of consciousness in which William James saw the means of a gentle and continuous shifting from one perception to another.

In Las Vegas, everything takes place as if the absence of any sense of belonging to the environment entailed a hypertrophied sensitivity to details. There is no possibility of visual escape into perceptual horizons of indeterminateness (left-right, forward-back, near-far), but, instead, only the pregnancy of enlarged, exaggerated and highlighted forms. Behind each lit-up sign no space is hollowed out, no incipient world. Everything is there, everything is flat. As thick as the giant advertising billboards that ubiquitously package it, loading it with naïve and comic symbols, crude, schematic messages, Las Vegas is a city of literal superficiality.

As we know, night vision habitually entails a loss of any sense of depth or distance, but in Las Vegas this physiological event is pushed to its sensory limits. Resembling the components of a Byzantine mosaic which might suddenly come to life but only to melt irreparably into one another, the artificial lights, made white by their own dazzle, beam out wildly like spotlights, and all seem to coexist upon a one-dimensional surface fixed before our eyes. Nothing any longer has a density or consistency, but each thing that emerges from the nocturnal backdrop floats like a ghost in a single space that refers to nothing other than itself. Tinged by the flashing radiance of the neon, below the flower bouquet-shaped *porte-cochere* of the Flamingo, one feels oneself to be a (dis)-integrating part of this live screen, a coloured hologram with neither thickness nor location.

Thus Las Vegas has the singular capacity to make us believe in our own unreality. In order to immerse us in a world of fantasy, it has understood that it must first of all deliver us from the world here on earth. This wrenching away from the real constitutes the precondition for being introduced into the world of pure fantasy. From this point of view artificial light and air-conditioning provide the perfect tools for a total de-realization of the self. They bathe us in a medium without any stability or contours where everything seems to be reduced to simple appearances. Unwittingly, Las Vegas performs something akin to a phenomenological reduction of the world around it, in the sense that it patiently empties each thing of its tangibility in order to transform it into pure manifestation. What is still held in the net of its unreality turns out ultimately to be mere show and it would be inappropriate to suppose that, behind this display of colours, lines and figures, there might be something substantial that would fill the void.

With its fever for perpetual change and its quest for novelty, which allow us to foresee in the short term the destruction and reconstruction of all the edifices which today make it famous, Las Vegas has no memory. Of course it has a brief history covering a century and a half, but this is not put forward by its promoters in their advertising or their attractions; instead it is well and truly relegated to oblivion. Thus nothing in the city commemorates the Paiute Indians, the first inhabitants of the region, nor the Spanish farmers who gave at its name, the Prairies, nor the Mormon colony that settled in the Valley in the late nineteenth century, thinking that they had at last found heavenly Sion, nor even less the resourceful, imaginative men of the Mafia (Siegel and Lansky) who transformed a mere rail-road town on the Los Angeles–Salt Lake City line into an oasis of gambling, loose living and luxury.

It is in the subdued lighting of the gambling rooms of the casino hotels, in these nowhere places, where nothing relates to life outside, thereby creating the true conditions of Utopia, that one grasps all the ontological ambiguity of Las Vegas at its keenest. Sometimes the illusion swallows up reality, the jovial collective snare becomes solidity and matter, because the attractions really do exist. This is in fact one of the sources of the pleasure of fantasy itself: it truly unfolds. Sometimes the town plays about with its own mirages so much that it seems to hold them at arm's length with a kind of tragic irony; however perfected and realistic these might be, they cannot compete with their own hallucinatory power, and then the very prestige of the trickery is denounced almost despite itself. Either the illusion feeds vampire-like on reality; or reality, itself born of the illusion, devalues all artifice which fails to reach the level of its own unreality. In other words, it could be that the real chimera that Las Vegas entails is the city itself, and not the countless artifices which make it up.

Neither far nor near, neither here nor anywhere else, Las Vegas marks itself out by nothingness. All the negative descriptions that can generally be used in labelling a city apply to it, for its absence of consistency actually makes its existence doubtful: no man's land, waste ground, non-place, ghost town, urban simulacrum, nowhere city, etc. For us it is Zeropolis, the non-city which is the very first city, just as zero is the very first number. The nothing that counts, the nothingness of neon. The degree zero city of urbanity, of architecture and culture, the degree zero city of sociability, art and ideas. The any-place town where everything begins again from zero, touching bottom and coming back up to the surface, with zeros piling up on a screen. A city of vacancy, of nothing and of absence, which nonetheless makes it a city. The city of *too much* which becomes *without*, of excess which turns into lack, of profusion which becomes privation. The city as atom and the atomic city, contradiction made the rule, architectural delirium and social confusion, Las Vegas tries one way or another to construct for itself an image of integrity, in constant opposition to the desert which everywhere encircles it and which reminds it unceasingly of its original vacuity.

Offerings to the Fun God

Every night, in Fremont Street, a sound and light spectacle is graciously provided courtesy of the consortium of neighbourhood casino owners. On a cylindrical vault 400 metres long and supported by eight steel pylons, hour after hour the show is repeated: rippling lightwaves, supersonic planes going by, dancing octagons. Necks craning upwards, at each sound, at each visual motif, the crowd exclaims, sometimes in between mouthfuls of soda, as if they are watching the birth of a new galaxy before their very eyes. Like frescoes dedicated to the Fun god, the flashing of 2,000 light bulbs roots the hundreds of passers-by to the spot in a pagan ecstasy, punctuated by a few cries of admiration which attempt to feign some genuine emotion. All by itself, this spectacle encapsulates the power of Las Vegas: 'a theology of profoundest mediocrity makes of every Saul a Paul.'[2]

The animated roof covering the whole of its length, 27 metres above it, turns the street in its garish envelope into a kind of neo-gothic cathedral. The central nave offers the main pictures in this story made of light and flashing shapes. Either side, instead of the customary stained-glass windows are the gaudy facades of the casinos, each, in its particular style, forming a votive chapel where offerings are made. *Urbi et orbi*, the city and the world united in an unusual synthesis: the fantastic dome of Fremont Street.

For the casino owners and those who devise the spectacle, there is one governing truism: the need to keep clients occupied 24 hours out of 24, with visual and sound attractions that are increasingly sensational, without leaving them any time to grasp what is happening to them. In their inclination to cram non-stop bustle into every iota of space and time lived through, it is as if they had a panic-stricken fear that 'someone, somewhere in Las Vegas, was going to be left with a totally vacant minute on his hands'.[3] There can be no doubt whatsoever that the Fremont Street experience is about this kind of *horror vacui*.

Here, one can only be amazed by the fact that the architectural principles of Gothic art, advocated by the builders of the Late Middle Ages, made manifest on the one hand in the transparency of surfaces in a film of light, and on the other the fusing of interior and exterior into an impression of limitlessness, should find their improbable fulfilment several centuries later in the soil of the New World, and there is no certainty of the spectacle being any less staggering than it was then in Chartres or Amiens, nor the message any less edifying. It is the same quest for a sensation of the diaphanous and oceanic, which, by virtue of sparkling flat colours and monumental figures, creates an emotional mood of participation in some whole that is greater than ourselves. Everything combines to produce this diffuse feeling of unreality. The concreteness of the materials is polarised by the luminosity of the digital images that run across the vault in a deafening racket that wipes out any possibility of concentration. Hardly any figurative images appear in the electronic spectacle itself, instead for most of the time it is a display of pure abstract forms.

When the digital Mass is over, the tide of gaping onlookers heads *mechanically* for the rows of fruit machines as if to continue their prayers and slip coins into these new charity boxes. Yet, one could not hope to extricate this religious experience from the profanity that shapes everyday life in Las Vegas if one did not devote oneself to the most exemplary and most sacred occupation that typifies this place: gambling.

Let us take for example the side street that leads us to Caesars Palace, the very first of the themed casinos, built by Melvyn Grossman at the start of the Sixties. In the middle of a basin, surrounded by a sugar pink colonnade which reminds us of the one in front of the basilica of St Peter's in Rome, a replica in Carrara marble of the Victory of Samothrace creates a unique visual landmark. Beneath the huge *porte-cochere* in aquamarine, a group of doormen, for once sober and assiduous, give us directions: a long moving walkway which brings us to the centre of the building. Crossing the threshold of a casino is a unique experience, at once philistine and primal. We leave behind the electric tinsel universe of the street to enter into a nocturnal world where at first sight we can hardly see a thing.

Lost in a fathomless night, all one notices to begin with is the terrible din of some machinery or other. We might almost have fallen into the cavern of Hephaestus. A noise of springs and bolts crashing together and pistons grinding hits you. Gradually, the darkness recedes along with the chaotic sound-scape, and a still indistinct decor composed of thousands of pale spotlights and polychrome crates becomes discernible. With a feeling of nonchalance about what is happening to us, we become aware that we are standing in the middle of a vast hall, with a fairly low ceiling and dim lighting, where hundreds of human bodies are lined up side by side, neither seeing nor speaking to one another, looking at coloured metal boxes where, upon the operation of an articulated arm, fruits, human figures and naïve pictures move about as if in a magic lantern. With mechanical reverberations on all sides, in search of a seat we proceed unthinkingly into the aisles packed with dozens of others like us. Groups of people bustle excitedly around gaming tables, blocking our way. Above them, huge letters running across digital screens are reminiscent of some strange language.

But little by little things we can identify begin to stand out. Upon a dais surmounted by a pediment in pinkish stucco, dominating what appears to be the main entrance, Julius Caesar and Cleopatra, no less, lie on their sides in a languid pose, greeting those who pass with a gesture of would-be

majesty. Whether or not the effect is intentional, they bear a striking resemblance to film actors in some epic of ancient Rome. As far as historical accuracy is concerned, these imitations have no real aspirations. Roman legionaries stand guard either side of columns that run all three Greeks styles together, in a muddle that would have Vetruvius thoroughly perplexed. They adopt the brutish demeanour of those who are hardened to anything that might happen. Sometimes, for no apparent reason, they bring down their long spears in unison, blocking access to the hall, then, in a similarly inexplicable manner, they lift them again. Right now there are dancers flapping about on the platform, and musicians belting out the music for all they're worth, just as one might expect. We've arrived.

Yet it is quite a different show that holds our attention. In the gaming parlours with their subdued lighting, day merges with night in a featureless continuum. Deep inside the rooms laid out so that the gamblers have lost all spatial and temporal reference points – there are no signs for exits, no clocks anywhere – tarnished tokens are being fed mechanically into the slits of the slot machines by every kind of person America classifies as a deadbeat (poverty-stricken pensioners; obese and dowdily dressed black matrons; southern white trash there to gamble away their social security cheques; large parties of convention participants who have flown in to do some slumming on the cheap, etc.).

With feigned interest, these poor people, judging by their old clothes or, at any rate, their vacant eyes, watch the little windows in the slot machines and for hours on end they wait with no sign of emotion for the phoney coins to come clinking out. With a hand gloved to prevent calluses they pull on the one-armed bandit's arm, looking, as the writer Michael Ventura has unhesitatingly put it, 'dazed'. This is what comes of passion, or else habit. Take your pick. They are clamped to their stools, only pausing now and then to cast a furtive glance at their equally luckless neighbour before quickly resuming their task. Others, just as wordlessly, wander about the aisles carrying their little plastic buckets, generously provided by the casino, their purpose to gather up unlikely future winnings, like incontinent invalids trailing around with their chamber pots in the lifeless precincts of a sanatorium.

From everywhere and out of nowhere deafening sirens, aiming to imitate some well-known tune, will sometimes blare out from one of the rooms, and a shower of coins will come clattering down as they are meant to in this universe of total simulation, dropping round the feet of the happy winner and extracting maybe a mere syllable from his or her lips. Every five minutes, a waitress, supposedly sexy by the standards of the management, in a toga that is too short so that it exposes her too-flabby thighs, equipped with her regulation carotene-based, orange-hued fake tan and that archetypal smile that makes you worry about imminent facial paralysis, brings you a kind of transparent amphora containing a giant cocktail with a name you've never heard of, its peculiar colour and mixture being not without some correspondence to your mental state at the time as they sway about in the glass between the plastic palm tree and the sugar frosting.

Then, without overmuch conviction, we tell ourselves that it is time to participate in the ritual and offer up our mite. With no illusions, I feed quarters into the one-armed bandit's slot and pull the lever until it comes to a stop. Immediately the three screens come to life. Figures you can hardly make out run by quickly in a discontinuous ribbon to the tinkle of some out of date tune and, ten seconds later, they come to a halt with the verdict: an orange, a bunch of cherries and a sun. Still sitting there, I struggle to figure out the meaning of this visual oracle, but nothing else happens. I scour my memory for some link between these three symbols, to no avail. In my mind I try out two or three fresh possibilities, but there in front of us the images remain hopelessly mute. Then our neighbour on the right, without even turning, addresses us with the somewhat superior tone of an old hand who knows the drill: 'you've lost, buddy, you'd better have another go.'

Even if you make every effort to merge into the overexcited atmosphere of the place, you still can't stop yourself from experiencing a feeling of deep unease. All these people compulsively engaged in a repetitive and physically ridiculous task in which they don't even take any pleasure make you think of slave workers in some Southeast Asian sweatshop. The sadness probably derives from the contrast between the quantity of energy expended, in all innocence, in order to join in the party, and the signal poverty of the outcome. I'm not talking here just about financial poverty, for in the end the winners are few and far between and most of the gamblers are quite simply being relieved of the last of their savings, but of the poverty of what is experienced.

When all is said and done, the leisure and social experience offered by Las Vegas, with all its attractions and shows, casinos and cabarets, amounts to practically nothing in anyone's life. A fleeting excitement of the senses, a frenzy of buying and escapism that very quickly borders on persistent nausea. But it is significant that, despite its capacity to induce rapid disgust, *the town that never sleeps* always manages to seduce the have-nots and the suckers, the high rollers and the sharks. It seems even to be satisfied in the end with this status as a superficial, shallow town. It has to be said that on this void it has built an empire.

Graveyard of Signs

In the yard behind the Boneyard, at the gates of the desert, old neon signs that have seen long service are piled up, waiting to be put back together some day in a place just for them, or more likely to be destroyed in an illicit dumping ground. One after the other, the bright lights have gone out, and here they spend a golden retirement, like 70-year-olds in Florida, dazed by the sun, burned up with boredom. Under the combined effect of heat and damp-free air, they never rust, but age almost intact, safely out of sight, without losing any of their fresh-paint looks. Except for just one thing. Thousands of electric bulbs, deprived of their vital fluid, heat up in the sun and sometimes suddenly explode with a little pop like a bone snapping. In this chaos of signs, we can pick out the Aladdin's lamp that sat on the roof of the eponymous casino. The only wish it now contains is to find a place soon in a museum that will preserve its fragile cracked beauty. Yet from these untimely carcasses, lying close together in a disordered muddle, there emanates a strange impression of harmony.

The more their value as indicators has faded, the more their value as exhibits becomes apparent. Freed from their showy commercial effects, they appear for the first time in their formal beauty, in their painstaking calligraphy. No longer electric monsters who, like hundreds of Medusa heads, petrify passers-by into immobility, but steel flowers with delicate curves, Henry Moore sculptures circled with fluorescent diadems. With use extinguished, form takes over and is revealed as pure appearance, with no end or purpose: a play of light and curves, a beauty that is free and conceptless, *pulchritudo vaga*. In the open air, the names and numbers become writing unimpelled to signify, on the white page of a sky that is immensely blue.

Even dusty and falling apart, these abandoned signs still have a touch of refinement. It would be a pity to see them as nothing more than the relics of a market and consumer culture born in the 1950s, because, by virtue of their iconic power, which synthesises part of the city's history, they stand as real artistic creations, and, eventually recognised as such, would not disgrace a museum of Pop Art. In this derelict place, this dumping ground without electricity, they begin to lead a new life, one that is calmer and more discreet.

Now that their symbolic effect has receded, the signs return to their original nature as works, signs of things. They are uncovered in a different light, the one imagined by the sculptor the day that he conceived of them, the electrograph that shaped their giant letters, colossal and yet delicate, their incandescent fullnesses and slender upstrokes. Even if these are just dismembered bodies or the vestiges of a bygone past, we tell ourselves that this, the neon sign cemetery of the Boneyard, is not where the true ghosts do their haunting. Thirstlessly, they sip at frosted margaritas in the air-conditioned casinos that are not far away.

The Double-sided Face of Utopia

'The Circus Circus is what the whole hep world would be
doing on Saturday night if the Nazis had won the war.'
Hunter S. Thompson
Fear and Loathing in Las Vegas

'Anything for anybody' is the philosophical watchword of Las
Vegas that will never feature on any of its publicity brochures.
But certainly not *anyhow*. Behind the architectural anarchy
accentuated by the geographical discord of each hotel casino
which, simultaneously, opens out onto the street to draw
clients inside and lives enclosed within a strictly self-referen-
tial space, there reigns a non-stop surveillance of people's
movements and actions. This domination of the environment
is apparent right from the start in the structure of each
building, each street attraction or illuminated sign which
imposes a certain reading of the town and leaves no possible
room for idle strolling or for any revision of sense, whether this
be direction or meaning.

The impression of sheer frenzy and the reality of surveillance are combined to give rise to an urban space in which the
lack of visible boundaries competes with the presence by
stealth of a very well-developed strategy of subduing individ-
uals. An incongruous city where unintended incongruity has
no place, a city of so-called fantasy where the marginal and the
anomalous are absolutely banned by the private police of the
casinos who relentlessly oversee the order of things. Each
movement of the city is in any case spied upon by an extremely
complex system of video cameras which scan nearly 90 per

cent of the downtown area and the Strip, according to the municipality's security experts, who take pride in this figure.

Once you've left the casino and hotel district, Las Vegas resembles any other American city, with its low urban density and its endless residential suburbs. But there too, inconspicuously, a logic of security shapes the pattern of property occupancy. With the highest urban expansion in the USA over the last ten years, Las Vegas has seen the growth of 'gated communities' on its periphery, with detached homes in vast high-security areas where your credentials have to be checked by heavily armed watchmen guarding entrance gates that resemble the way into medieval cities. Hidden behind high, often barbed-wire, walls, well away from the hysterical excesses of downtown – which are frequently inflated by the paranoid logic of high-security thinking – these new suburban communities are organized for peace and quiet, around a golf course, a swimming pool and tennis courts. As Mike Davis observes: 'The security-driven logic of urban enclavization finds its most popular expression in the frenetic efforts of Los Angeles's affluent neighbourhoods to insulate home values and lifestyles'.[4]

These private spaces are hermetic and inward looking, issuing the city with a blunt exclusion order. They reject all contact with the adjacent urban environment, and any intrusion from outside is immediately identified as a threat. In their fear of promiscuity and exchange, they turn back in on the community, protected as it is in its carapace of surveillance systems, seeing it as a healthy body that the city can only infect, corrupt and poison. Suburban but lacking in urbanity, of the city but uncivic, gated communities establish themselves in the city while contesting its essential ways of being (exchange, movement, visibility). This impugning of any minimal solidarity with civic space is expressed for example in their attempts to seek exemptions from municipal levies and taxes. Far from being indicative of a malaise, this secession from the city is

experienced as some kind of positive discrimination, a voluntary incarceration behind the bars of state-of-the-art video cameras.

Cheap utopias for the middle classes, garden cities turned into Fort Knox, these secessionist private areas, which proliferate on the edges of Las Vegas in the neighbourhoods of Lakes and North Henderson, are more like fantasies of a self-sufficient community rather than actually forming any real human collectivity. Based on shared interest rather than identification, they simulate the inwardness of a small pastoral society, but they have no illusions about the company they seek out. Deep inside these closed communities themselves there prevails a fear of neighbours, and the same mistrustful looks. The obvious reason is that, once freed from the external pressure of the group, the residents of gated communities are now at the total mercy of the everyday requirements of the homeowners' association and its internal regulations.

Not even public buildings are immune from this architecture of self-defence. One signal product of the suburban paranoia sweeping through Las Vegas is the Clark County Governmental Center, a beige-brown edifice set right in the middle of the desert and easily mistaken for a bunker. With its massive steel-edged and starkly unembellished cubes, its narrow windows that look exactly like fortress loopholes, it comes out of the purest security-conscious aesthetic that flourishes in California and Florida, those sunshine states where people opt for private high-security development neighbourhoods. So side by side in Las Vegas, just a few miles apart, one finds urban frenzy and voluntary prisons, a fondness for architectural excess and a preference for sober and intimidating buildings, almost military in aspect, which reprove those who dare to look at them with 'No Trespassing' warnings. However, there should be no mistake, it is the same concern to combine desire with security that in one place builds the casinos and in another the gated communities.

In fact, the casino hotels constitute the original forms of the privatization of public space. These are enclosed and codified enclaves in which everything is organized with a rigour that leaves nothing to chance, unless it be chance itself. In the world of gambling, nothing can really be a gamble. No shifts or uncertainties in human and social relationships. Everything is programmed, from the combinations of the numbers on the cylindrical vault of the Fremont Street Experience, which can be seen at a distance of more than 400 yards, to the distribution of the ladies' toilets in the Luxor, more than 18 feet underground. Here, enjoyment never leaves any room for improvisation. The childlike exaltation that treads the pavements of the Strip, the frantic buzz of excitement around the backgammon tables and the slot machines, the pseudo-libertine frenzy of the risqué shows for the titillation of old goats, is all strictly overseen, kept in check and codified, despite the wild appearance of Babylonian disorder and abandonment. Thus Las Vegas stands as a utopia in its two essential aspects: the realization of personal desire through the rationalization of social relations. It is, at one and the same time, the town where all desires can be fulfilled and where a strict regimentation of space gives this perfect satisfaction the total guarantee of not being disturbed or interrupted.

There are in fact innumerable indications leading us to believe that a Utopia, in the Renaissance formulation of Thomas More or Tommaso Campanella, does not consist merely of a non-place outside geography and history, where the political and affective human passions can be fulfilled unchecked and without violence as the fancy takes them. It just as much represents a transhistorical space where social regulation achieves an unparalleled rationality and efficacy. This is because the utopia, through its fondness for the ideal and the normative, sets its sights on a double challenge: to eliminate all forms of incoherence in social, intellectual and affective relations so as to allow free rein to the now finally unrepressed desires of each person; to build a homogeneous society in accordance with a consistent and uncontestable order which preordains in every detail all possible relations between human beings. A *Janus Bifrons* (two-faced Janus), it argues in favour of the total satisfaction of desires in a society of endless abundance wherein every contradiction will have been resolved, and at the same time it padlocks these satisfied appetites into a regulated ordering which no longer leaves any room for the unusual or the discordant.

It is this new synthesis of pleasure and submission which fundamentally determines the whole life of Las Vegas. It is manifestly expressed in the constant infantilization of its citizens and its guests. Infantile clothes, infantile food, infantile behaviour. It is as if the city wanted to experience a perpetual childhood. But what kind of childhood is this? Is it the mischievous childhood of learning about life? Is it the childhood of private dreams and discoveries made about other people? Definitely not. First and foremost, it is about giving primacy only to one's whims. For Tom Wolfe, this 'childlike megalomania' of Las Vegas is conveyed exactly in the attitude of the child who pleads 'Don't make me go to bed'. It is puerility, rather than youthfulness, that now influences every aspect of ordinary life. The process of regression seems virtually widespread. Gambling, which is to be found in every form and in every place, even in the toilets of McCarran Airport, is linked to this precise social combination of happy satisfaction and unerring supervision sought by the child. Gambling means wanting to achieve satisfaction by renouncing any responsibility for changing the world.

Just like a child enjoying his or her irresponsibility all the more while safe in the knowledge that the adults are watching over him, the gambler in Las Vegas submits quite willingly to his or her uninhibited pleasure being externally regulated. His jovial insouciance is a mask that is really hiding the seriousness with which he decides for now to sacrifice all the richness of his life for the sake of having plenty of fun. Unable to take the personal risk of living for himself in terms of spontaneous excitement, his desire to be accepts the social compromise of self-censorship in the form of conventional pleasures regulated by others, with the outward excessiveness of these ultimately of a piece with his complete alienation from those who, while not being players, lay down the rules. In this coercive aspect, playfulness has as its object the domestication of that original desire without an object which flows in the veins of every one of us, by imposing on it the directive forms of the theme park. It aims to channel vitality and make it into something that is no more than alive: a rictus of joy.

Moreover, the fun which, in all its forms, becomes constantly part and parcel of the average American's everyday life, represents this complex and underhand process which gives to the necessary expenditure of his or her joyful vitality the pre-drawn configuration of a socially decreed jollity. This means that the more intense the pleasures brought by the game, the stronger the subordination to it becomes. The policy of the quid pro quo of entertainment, which for 50 years has determined the urban and social crux of Las Vegas, represents the extreme tip of this social domestication, which is freely consented to and leaves it up to the subdued individual to draw his or her own conclusions about this freely undertaken enslavement: that it has been enjoyable.

Of course, not every player is compelled to play. They can sit the game out or take their chips back. But what happens when all their options in life, even the most mundane (shopping for food, stopping for gas) have to be fun, forcing them to participate endlessly and unreservedly, in some kind of obligatory mirth, in games that are increasingly more stupid, and forcing them to become the comedy of their own situation? And what happens to their natural joyful vitality, when the models of play that are on offer, not to say prescribed, and which generally require the submission of the participants to codes that they cannot alter without their total curtailment, little by little impregnate the whole of their social and political life?

Within this double tendency towards the security of desire and the desire for security, Las Vegas stands as a utopia in a strict sense of the word.[5] Like its precursors on paper, it excoriates all social and political contradictions in an apparent urban and visual incoherence. With an exemplary sense of nit-picking regulation, it cuts out all amorous, vital and playful passions whose unstable nature might come to threaten social cohesion, either within the fairytale bastions of the casinos or in the grey fortresses of the gated communities. This is why the paranoid urbanity of Las Vegas is in the end rife with the idea that fantasy, in its highest sense of desire as an ideal, can only be realized at the cost of its perfect appeasement to a harsh order which alone makes it possible. It seems to be telling those who are able to hear its messages: 'you can only fulfil your deepest desires by doing so in accordance with the prescribed manner. You must then renounce the insecurity of natural desire for a guarantee of socially assured satisfaction.' It is therefore not surprising to observe that escape and imprisonment are combined there in a space where desire mystifies itself by giving up the 'cursed part' of the risk that constitutes it, in order to enter into an immediate bargain contract with the norms of graded wishes and happiness under military protection. What this comes down to is that Las Vegas, with its consummate talent for fake pleasures, links passion with regulation, opulence with normalization, and the land of Cockayne with a totalitarian universe.

The Profusion of Resemblances

At the wheel of a hired car, I drive slowly along the Strip until I reach downtown. What I see is a succession of motels, service stations and vast parking facilities that stretches on and on. It's as if a loop of advertising spots had become embedded in the buildings. Either side of the road, giant signs rise in an uninterrupted line, lighting up like the architectural embodiment of the fitful ebb and flow of those going by.

Behind this mural patchwork of digital images, which merge into one another by dint of their intent to be conspicuous, stand the even more flashy casino hotels, with their crudely constructed attempts to encapsulate human history on some chosen theme from antiquity to Futureworld at the level of a six-year-old child. At first you can hardly see them, because they are so big, but from further away they become manifest in their individuality. They form the real landscape of Las Vegas, they are its emblems: the black pyramid and the gilded sphinx of the Luxor, the princess's castle of the Excalibur, the Manhattan of New York New York, etc. Unlike other cities in the world, the capital of gambling cannot be epitomized by just one or two recognizable elements. Instead it multiplies them in a profusion, as if thereby aiming to transcend for once and all the possibility of being assigned any lasting identity. To take the measure of the dozens of huge casino hotels along the strip, you have to leave your car and melt into the human procession that goes past them.

On the pavements or the parking lots that follow disconnectedly one after the other, there wanders a featureless and compact crowd devoid of any nonchalance (aimless strolling is

frowned on here). Its forward progress is interrupted only by young people clad in sportswear who, in peremptory fashion, hand out advertising fliers giving the addresses of erotic shows, money-off vouchers for nearby supermarkets, or free tickets for a champagne breakfast at the Sahara or the Stardust. Surprised by this intrusion of the routine into a world of fantasy, most people don't even bother to look at these and discard them at once. Carried by the strong wind that gusts between the compact masses of the hotel blocks, the leaflets and handouts blow away, stick to the legs of the passers-by and end up strewn on the ground.

The street quickly becomes dirty and then, as if roused from a dream by this interference of the sordid into a self-styled magical world, you notice that the showy architectural splendours coexist with the topological poverty of areas which are presumably under construction. Between each complex, a haven of glittering prosperity, lie poorly lit stretches of waste ground, half-finished or abandoned buildings which immediately bring to mind a city devastated by war. Thus the Strip becomes an alternation of palaces and building-site huts, palm trees and mechanical diggers. Most of the time, even the pavements are in a state of disrepair; here and there the tarred surface of the roadway has burst open, and iron sheeting covers up the deep potholes that riddle it. Once the heady effect of the neon lights and the all-night bustle has worn off, one's eyes are opened to surroundings so shabby they rather take the shine off the swanky image Las Vegas would like to claim for itself. Faced with this spectacle of mediocrity, I recall Nick Tosches' observation in *The Holy City*:

> Dante did not write in the age of malls, but he would have recognised Las Vegas, in any age, for what it is: a religion, a disease, a nightmare, a paradise for the misbegotten.[6]

Despite these far from brilliant juxtapositions, which make the city itself a bastard, born of the illicit love affair between the lustrous and the vulgar, the crowd of unaccustomed walkers goes on its way without grumbling. It makes a stop at each casino, almost surprised at being able to get around like this on foot. It stands for a moment under the light-drenched awnings, then the groups that detach themselves make a decision either to go into the casinos after a satisfactory security check, or to continue their walk. The Stations of the Cross, minus the cross and the stations. Just this irrepressible urge, at all costs, to be a part of whatever is supposed to matter, to be a must. Not wanting to miss out on anything, for there is always something going on somewhere and they have to be there. To *be there* rather than to *be*.

All around me, garish swirls of colour are reflected in the gleaming bodywork of the cars, luminous eighteen-feet high letters hanging in the sky by some unknown means block the uniformly midnight-blue horizon, there are glowing billboards that suddenly blaze, advertising signs that come to life and wave hello, road signs that join in too, bombarding your vision, subjugating it with a violence that becomes quite blindingly excessive. A city that literally zaps you in the eye. The tired retina hurts from so much nervy information to cope with in such a short time, in such a cramped space.

Apart from the flashing animation of the street, not very much really happens. There are no hawkers, no kiosks, no public gardens. Apart from the people on them, the pavements are relatively empty, stripped bare, as if just hosed down. Even under the open sky, it's like being in a shopping mall where you see nothing of a city except for its commercial side. When they are not congregating around a casino or some official attraction, the tourists walk on calmly, without letting their excitement or their boredom show. This is probably the effect of the heat, which, even after nightfall, is still stifling, inducing a certain floppy relaxation. Between the Mirage and the Treasure Island, passers-by are misted with little jets of water whose sprinklers are loosely hooked on to the steel shingles of the roof. People hardly have time to catch the moisture before the water evaporates into a damp haze. Children naughtily slip back past them to repeat the experience but already some other city attraction grabs their attention.

Now the crowd is packed in front of the Mirage for the volcanic eruption that happens every quarter of an hour. A rumbling sound announces that the explosion is about to take place. Tongues of flame suddenly burst out of the crater, while the first streams of vaporous lava are already gushing down its sides (this is red smoke, and somewhat unconvincing even to eyes as conciliatory as mine after these hours of nocturnal wandering). Next, the pool surrounding the smoking cone flares up. To the uncontained joy of an audience that laps up every detail, everything occurs exactly as programmed by the central computer, hour on hour, day in day out. This lurid outpouring never alters in the slightest. Yet the only thing which really manages to make an impact on my somewhat numbed sensibility, after such long exposure to the city, turns out to be the smell of burnt petroleum that poisons the air.

Were I to stay here for months, surveying every nook and cranny of the town, joining in all its festivities and official events, and feasting my eyes unreservedly on its preposterous trash, I doubt whether I would learn anything more than what my first impressions tell me. Once what hits you in the first few hours has faded, the city very quickly becomes wearisome. There is little to see beyond the casinos and the themed hotels, and even less to do. All the shows are essentially alike, variations on amusement park fare. Admittedly, sundry enticements of all kinds abound. On every street corner, touts from the huge entertainment complexes adjoining the casinos offer excursions on paddle steamers; rides in stagecoaches from the days of the Wild West pursued by a horde of genuine Apaches appropriately howling and gaudily daubed with warpaint; an aerial sightseeing trip to the Grand Canyon by helicopter, with a champagne breakfast on the Canyon's rim. But in the end it is all so much sensational overkill that you wind up with a feeling of utter stupefaction.

The local population itself seems resigned to taking uniformity for granted. Whether they go to see a nightclub revue or a boxing match, whether they bet on how many winning shots Alan Iverson will score at the next basketball game against the New York Knicks, or sit down at the roulette or the craps table, or try striking up a conversation with the barman dressed as a centurion at Caesars Palace, everyone involved seems to alternate between bursts of canned laughter and a facial chill that can only be accounted for by too much air conditioning. Even if you really try to break through that straitjacket of oversimplified behaviour, the perennial have-a-nice-day smile, every time you try to take a conversation further by appealing to personal feelings, not just conventional opinions, you meet with a wall of indifference, as if the violence of the desert environment had transformed the inhabitants of Las Vegas into a thing bereft of humanity: a rock, a cactus, a cloud.

Behind the Scenes

Every half hour or so, large metal boxes with smoked windows that mirror the space around them arrive from the four corners of the land at the Las Vegas Greyhound terminus. They pull up in a screeching of brakes and thereupon decant their consignment of hollow-eyed pilgrims, who become lost in a cloud of dust and smoke, sweat and gas fumes which immediately catches in the throat.

Without a single word, with no sign of admiration or disgust, the half-conscious travellers totter around reclaiming their suitcases tied with string and their plastic bags stuffed with the few essential objects they are persuaded no human existence can do without. It is 12.25. They have just spent two or three days travelling across the United States by bus, most of them from the East, or to be more exact, from the small towns of the Midwest and the South, with nothing to occupy them on the way except counting the cars with registration plates from their home state. Right now, they hardly bother to take note of their surroundings, but head straight for the building which they will immediately hurry out of after rapidly quenching their thirst at the water fountain. In the unshadowed brightness of noon, they advance blindly towards the invisible city which holds out its arms either to embrace them or beat them black and blue.

Thus in Las Vegas there coexist two types of people in superficial harmony: the gamblers and the dealers. For those who backbreakingly apply themselves to losing their money, the town presents itself as a pleasant vacation spot, completely occupied with making people voluntarily part with their money and transmuting it almost magically into a nostalgic but happy feeling: 'I let myself be taken to the cleaners.' But for the others, those who endlessly busy themselves ungraciously around the listless tourists slumped on their stools in front of a one-armed bandit, those who tramp back and forth for miles delivering insipid cocktails, those who open the same door with the same contraction of the facial muscles a thousand times in a row, those who hand out money-off vouchers in the street, the 'city that never sleeps' shows itself in quite a different light. It drains all your energy, disturbs your balance, and in the end it chews you up and spits you out. Beneath the bonhomie of its acknowledged absurdity and its unperturbed, thriving vulgarity, the city can harbour a cruelty beyond belief. This may well be accentuated by the extreme harshness of the desert climate: the torrid heat, the virtual absence of cooling winds in the evening, the desolate and inhospitable natural surroundings. When someone comes here not for gambling or entertainment, but to work, there is only one priority: to forge a carapace so hard that it can resist the dust and the imbecility. There is no other choice but to succumb to the extreme savagery of the most total benightedness, to surrender to it completely, to wallow in it with neither joy nor regret, and to hope, when all is said and done, that you will find your sole salvation in some preordained way out: by setting up your own business, whatever it may be (a wedding chapel, a motel, an erotic nightclub).

Psychotropic Urbanity

No one does it better.
Las Vegas motto

America's adventure playground. Las Vegas, the old haunt of the *famiglia*, has become in just a few years the favourite spot of American families. They come to the Nevada Desert essentially to have a good time and to find their own share of that 'neon dust' that makes life sparkle and, when the trip is over, provides some happy memories. The city itself is nothing but a gigantic non-stop spectacle. The postcard has absorbed the whole reality and spat it back out pretty quickly in the form of thinly processed psychedelic icons for the middle classes: extreme sensations that are obtained by safe, legal and inoffensive means. A trip on the Strip, but within the confines of the licit. An extreme adventure without danger, total excitement without anxiety and the absolute thrill without any fear, that sums up the ultimate social discrimination produced by America.

The ideal Las Vegas customer resembles Raymond, an engineer from Phoenix and an unrepentant gambler, still sitting at a craps table at half past three in the morning, as described by Tom Wolfe in February 1964 in his reportage piece on Las Vegas for *Esquire* magazine:

He was also enjoying what the prophets of hallucinogen call 'consciousness expansion'. The man was psychedelic. He was beginning to isolate the components of Las Vegas' unique bombardment of the senses.

If you like playing the game of comparing generations, you can then say that the amusement parks with their orgies of technology and their myriad of fantasy extravaganzas have succeeded, where, at the level of an entire community, those values the hippies and protesters of the Sixties lived by have failed. All the same, the Las Vegas experience, and its neon test, has achieved clear success well beyond the psychedelic experiences of Ken Kesey's Merry Pranksters. And, in quantitative terms, it is much more effective than any attempts at supplying hallucinations by artificial means. When, in *Fear and Loathing in Las Vegas*, Hunter Thompson decided to mark the historic moment when the hippy era of flower power came to an end by drifting aimlessly around the gambling capital, it was precisely because Las Vegas, with its bogus proprieties, releases a hallucinogenic potency that is definitely stronger than any drug Timothy Leary might concoct. 'No, this is not a good town for psychedelic drugs. Reality itself is too twisted.'[7] By virtue of its visual and environmental delirium, its non-stop electrochemical drug, Las Vegas really does make drug-taking absurd, because of its sensory poverty. It turns the Sixties druggies into pale, over-cerebral imitations by comparison with the customer slumped in front of the slot machine in a themed casino.

As if unconsciously countering the Sixties protest movement, and the ethics of unreality it contained, on its own ground, American society has recycled this wish for a total destabilizing of meanings, but has given it a hygienic social value: entertainment. With an indisputable talent for recuperation, it has kept the idea of a critique of everyday banalities, but has at one and the same time endowed it with the form of a simple recourse to collective fantasy limited to a given space and time: the amusement park, the themed hotel, etc. The utopian has been downgraded to the virtual. Whereas then the taking of hallucinogenic substances meant a denial of surrounding reality and therefore, even in its sometimes tragic outcome, had a critical potential, the experience of Las Vegas has reduced the distortion of the real to a mere game which, far from raising any objection to the social order, reveals its capacity to produce dreams, fantasies and imaginary life on an industrial scale.

Now the whole of America shoots up fun without any fear or remorse, happily injecting great bucketfuls of visual attractions into its veins with sterilized syringes in the form of special glasses for seeing in three dimensions, or stereo headsets that will give them multisensory contact with white whales. The experience of limits within the limits of experience, this is the subtle combination concocted by the industry of the spectacle. A frenzy of shapes and sensations, but one restrictively devised and managed. The engineers and producers of the firms that deliver the laser or digital shows have very quickly grasped that the 'doors of perception' open much more widely on roller-coasters a thousand feet off the ground, bombarded with hard rock and breathtaking pyrotechnic effects, than with a simple tab of LSD or mescaline.

Bit by bit, the Las Vegas techno-democracy of fun has perfected its hard (albeit harmless) drugs, which work directly on the nervous system through electro-visual stimulation, and which heal social wounds in a much deeper way than any other narcotic. The new amusement parks and the casino hotels have altered the flower power generation's quest for a physical ecstasy that lifts things out of the ordinary, for a collective opening to a new kind of holistic experience, for a unique moment that would give sense to the rest of our lives, into being swept along as spectators into some irreversible electronic version of sensory shock. Las Vegas has translated the artificial paradises into Edens of artifice. With a great deal of manipulation and advertising, it has turned the transcendence of the banal into a commerce, and turned the marvellous into a trade. This hallucinatory power of Las Vegas is such that the neo-hippies who nowadays parody the counterculture of the Sixties and meet up every summer in the northern Nevada Desert for a wild party they call 'Burning man', are unknowingly reproducing the rules of the amusement parks and themed casinos, through their very subversion. Contradiction is still imitation.

For all the promoters of entertainments and attractions in Las Vegas, it is therefore now a matter of observing a single law: offer the visitors and the tourists *experiences*. It is no longer enough to watch a show, even with participation, one needs to be having an experience, to become the show *in toto* oneself, the director of one's own entertainment. From an ordinary meal in a themed restaurant to immersion in an atomic submarine, via the chance of spending an evening and a hundred dollars to play a bit part in your favourite television series (which happens to be Star Trek, on the top floor of the Stratosphere Tower), everything is just an experiment, everything has to be the alibi for an unforgettable event. Probably regarding the customers' souls as a *tabula rasa*, the creators of Las Vegas have made up their minds to subject it to a total war consisting of violent impressions and limitless surprises. None the less the Blitzkrieg of spectacle must always go on being fun.

Quite shamelessly, fun, a word that is almost impossible to pin down, combines hysterical exaggeration and emotional limpness. The particular colour of a convertible hood is fun, a particular mimic of the robot clown at the Circus Circus is fun, a particular joke told by the croupier at the Stardust is fun. But it is very hard to explain what fun is in itself. Perhaps what Americans mean by fun is some kind of strange but relatively common sensation in which a sudden exaltation alternates with a passivity which doesn't lead to anything. At any rate it isn't just mild fleeting enjoyment, because fun actually requires some total investment by the individual which, for all that, leaves no memory.

Now if we take the time to observe what is really experienced in Las Vegas in terms of actions and deeds, we have to note that this experience is exceptional particularly for its brevity: it is reduced to the almost unreal moment of immediate

54

feeling. A violent, wild and instantaneous experience, with neither *experientia* nor *experimentum*, and where what is in strict terms empirical disappears all at once into some chimerical form: *res ficta*. An experience confined to the shock of the sudden impression without any time to settle slowly into thought or feeling, to let itself be felt or to become extended into a new memory, but disappearing as soon as it appears, like some flash of the senses that is as intense as it is forgotten, like a stimulus without any response, where the absence of reaction only flows into some new discharge.

In this living laboratory of gambling and entertainment, the spectacle in its old form as the show is now completely over and done with, and belongs to the anachronistic days of separation and distance. The product of a new era is the spectacle of virtual, integrative interaction, of direct experiences *in media res*, which will leave us a violent but fleeting imprint, a dramatic impact on the skin, a wound of pleasure which will make each of us say: *I was there.*

Ghost Town

Around Las Vegas, off the beaten tourist tracks, are derelict old motels in their death throes, choked with weeds and small sand dunes in the process of formation. The clapped-out sign casts its huge shadow against the few walls that are still standing. The porte cochere with its flaking paint has partly caved in and the debris lies on the ground blocking access to the entrance hall, which is covered in indecipherable graffiti and obscene slogans.

It feels strange to be looking at the ruins of buildings which were precisely not meant to last. Because of some peculiar reversal, these commercial structures which had been built with the aim of meeting a temporary need, now express an architectural value which they absolutely lacked in the past. By their simple transformation into rubble, these ruins of the ephemeral, these rickety vestiges of a vernacular architecture, almost magically acquire a lived temporality which had been refused them. If it is true that time possesses a formative power, the ruin then turns the motel into a building at the point when it has, paradoxically, ceased to exist. Its decay is its opportunity. Only its irreversible deterioration can bring about its metamorphosis into real architecture, placing it within the irrevocable order of historical works. Thanks to its decrepitude, the motel gains humanity for the first time in its banal existence, thereby attaining a meaning of its own, in the display of its complete loss of function.

The Transfiguration of Banality

There will soon come a time when the turquoise blue of the facade of Binion's Horseshoe will become the focus of a more profound aesthetic sensation than any effect of surface colour in a painting by Tintoretto. In the aesthetic temperament of our successors, its oblong forms and glass and steel corset will replace the Gothic triptychs and Baroque golds of the past. All the casinos will be subject to the same artistic shift.

Las Vegas will be visited like the Louvre or the National Gallery, with the same exaggerated respect for the genius of our ancestors. With the scant difference that Las Vegas will be its own open-air museum.

People will bow before the display cases that put on show the glittering relics which the Society of the Spectacle at the end of the second millennium came to leave behind. They will read with interest the notices on the wall telling us what great men Liberace and Jay Sarno were. Every museum in the world will want to build up its own collection of neon tubes and illuminated signs, will want to have a section labelled *Las Vegas*, full of old slot machines, sugar pink stucco fountains, huge *porte-cocheres*, just as others today have their Coptic or Phoenician sections. Every museum will have its glitz and glamour department, that has its smartly turned out curators with a serious look about them. As you hurry through the vast subterranean halls of the casinos, as you breathlessly follow the countless spectacles of sound and light, as your glance shifts about continually, you sometimes have the impression that, beneath its uncontrollable bustle, the museum mummification of Las Vegas has already begun.

Fiat Lux

All of Las Vegas comes down to its lights. By day, the limpid light of the desert irradiates the town with a perfect transparency. Because of the low humidity in the air, everything looks like new, with sharp, clean cut edges. There is no hazy hint of white to blur their contours. On the contrary, buildings and people alike, no matter how far away, stand out with such clear definition that they seem to correspond to their individual essences.

At night, the huge neon illuminations that light up the sky of Las Vegas have no trouble supplanting the stars that shine in its firmament. Beneath a deluge of shifting colours that fancifully sculpt the street's solid elements into new shapes, the signs prevail like antique goddesses who are simultaneously protective and disturbing. Immaterial and transcendent, the neon light cannot but evoke some experience of divinity. But, unlike its biblical predecessor, the glittering beam of light from the electronic machinery does not tell us who made it.

The unknown artists who created the giant signs at the Sands, the Sahara and the Stardust are called Hermon Boernge, Jack Larsen and Kermit Wayne. The people who gave life to the artificial light which, in Las Vegas, emphasizes every word, every brand, have remained paradoxically in the shadow of the real estate promoters. It took Tom Wolfe, in the article already cited, to pay them homage and be grateful to them for having lit up our lives. One sign among thousands of others especially caught his attention, or rather his imagination: the bouquet of flowers on the Flamingo:

Such colours! All the new electrochemical pastels of the

Florida littoral: tangerine, broiling magenta, livid pink, incarnadine, fuchsia demure, Congo ruby, methyl green, viridine, aquamarine, phenonsafranine, incandescent orange, scarlet-fever purple, cyanic blue, tessellated bronze, hospital-fruit-basket orange. And such signs! Two cylinders rose at either end of the Flamingo — eight storeys high and covered from top to bottom with neon rings in the shape of bubbles that fizzed all eight storeys up into the desert sky all night long like an illuminated whisky-soda tumbler filled to the brim with pink champagne.

With night illumination by neon (red) and argon (blue), contained in different coloured glasses to give the signs every possible shade of colour, the town turns into the scene of a rock concert, with no free entrance and no star, no audience or podium. It reflects nothing. There is no mirror effect produced on its building facades. Instead, it *monopolizes* the ambient reality with its continual luminosity. Like huge strobe lights sweeping relentlessly across the space, the signs spurt out of the night, and with their brilliant but unsung dazzle, they paint the buildings, streets and passers-by in sugar pink or indigo blue. Artificial light is instantaneous and diffuse, simultaneously here and elsewhere. It washes over every single thing and drips on to the horizon. When it becomes the primary element in the cityscape, as in Las Vegas, it accentuates, if there was any need, the immateriality of the city and its inhabitants. And yet it never occurs to anyone to call it the 'city of light' or 'radiant city'.

Storm effects controlled by central computers, neon lightning tearing at the digital sky, with the sound of electronic thunder. All spatial distance is abolished, the past and future alike flow into the eternal present of the empty moment of surprise, of the shock that anaesthetizes through its over-intensity. Nowhere else other than in Las Vegas do we see such a profusion of neon tubes. Even in the most out of the way spots on the Strip, they beam out their phosphorescence with prodigality. But it is hard to believe that these garments of light really do cover soft bodies. As it prompts Frances Anderton and John Chase to observe:

> By daylight the Caesars Palace complex resembles a women's prison in Teheran; by night it is the ultimate Las Vegas casino. A majestic turquoise colonnade leads to a lurid pink-lit porte-cochere.[8]

Throughout the night, the lights colonize the city, but they leave it hollow-eyed and resourceless in the morning. This immateriality of light, which remakes the buildings into a mobile extravaganza, also put us in mind of the immateriality of the money that engenders them in the neon tube factories of YESCO, Ad Art and Sign System Inc.

For any architect, from ancient Egypt to the Archigram projects, light has always been a divine prerogative, which confirms its celestial origin: it lights up everything without letting itself be seen. Like Aristotle's veil, it materializes a condition of invisibility into utter visibility. When, as in Las Vegas, it reaches this crowning state of dazzlement, it erases all the monochrome asperities of the real. In a number of instances, the Las Vegas designers have only recycled in the most prosaic manner the sundry seductive strategies used by Baroque artists in the churches of the Counter-Reformation, following on from the Council of Trent.

For the family groups of passers-by taking a walk along the Strip, the most common sensory experience is tantamount to a sudden hallucination which persists by being incessantly renewed. With each step they take, their eyes are assailed by signs and digital light shows, to such a degree that they wonder whether they are dreaming with their eyes open. But the overall hallucination is not restricted to mere visual effects. It is reinforced simultaneously by the mental incapacity of spectators to

make up their mind about the apparition thrust upon them and by the no less private desire they immediately feel to be fully aware of it by themselves. With instantaneous stupefaction, they have no resources at their disposal for distinguishing the real from the imaginary, since this is a universe where the most ordinary things are the most improbable. By imitating the real, the imaginary does not replace it in terms of the logic of the artefact, but offers itself as the sole referent. The overall phantasmagoria of the city as a whole, which begins in the corridors of the airport terminal, these being filled with slot machines and other kinds of electronic poker, forms the psychological conditions for a 'willing suspension of disbelief', to employ Samuel Taylor Coleridge's definition of fiction. One must beware of any ironies of distance. This is the basis of the primordial power of Las Vegas's hallucinatory spectacle: persuading us that we ought not refuse to believe in it.

At dusk, the town becomes an extravaganza of light. The night is clad in garish brilliance. The street lights go on and everywhere the glitter of neon begins. By its total visibility, it presents a kind of profane spectacle accessible to all. Unlike the stained-glass windows of Gothic cathedrals, confined to the almost enclosed space of the ambulatory, it blooms in sight of everyone, in the prosaic open space of the street. With this, the sacred space of celestial luminosity has literally exploded, opening inside out. By virtue of their double privilege as celestial and immaterial, neon lights thereby secularize the value of transcendence represented by artificial light in the Middle Ages. When Georges Claude took out the patent for the neon gas lamp early in the twentieth century, he was quite unsuspecting of the sublime gift he was bringing to the modern world.

Unlike other decorative features of the urban landscape (buildings, shop windows, billboards) that enhance the city when evening falls, neon has two exclusive qualities: brightness and movement. It shines and it flickers, it glitters and lights up. However, with neon, luminosity and mobility are not separate, they combine perfectly in the electrical functioning. In itself, neon's mobile luminosity is strange to say the least. It seems to be diffused by an alternating movement of expansion and contraction which is precisely what provokes that very characteristic twinkling.

By their regular winking on and off, neon lights more generally stand for the luminous pulsing of the city. Because of them, we no longer feel our pulse beat beneath our skin, instead we see it, we have a direct contact with it. It is displayed above the streets and on the facades of buildings. Neon lights turn the city's skin inside out and show it off, uncovering the artificial mechanism that gives it life. It is as if they are the sparkling veins in a giant body into which a phosphorescent fluid has been introduced. Its recurrent beams enable us to follow the vital fluid that circulates through the city, bringing it life and sweeping away its toxins. It oxygenates the city's muscles, cleans out its dark corners and spreads its photochromatic vitality. It is therefore no exaggeration to say that neon signs uncover the city's secret anatomy. Like public electrocardiograms, they tell us about its internal order, its state of health.

What is most amazing about the neon tube is to do with the inversion it sets up in our perceptual relation to the world. Usually, and this is something that figurative pictorial techniques have to answer for, we perceive bodies surrounded by a kind of slightly darker contour. Thus colour surfaces seem to be encircled by the black line of their circumference, fine though it may be. The outline defines the form by making it stand out from the smoothly coloured background. In images of neon signs, the relationship between the design and the colour is completely inverted. The colour no longer fills in the form defined by the design, but itself becomes the design, the contour and the form. It is fluorescent colour that makes its own design of different visible forms, detaching itself from a single dark background. In fulfilment of what Matisse pursued throughout his lifelong work by other means, the colour of neon lights here becomes line and outline, sculpting forms and representing words and things. For the most part, it is colour itself that traces the intended form of the figurative neon lights adorning the streets and roadways, the dark interior hole standing for the background space. Quite the opposite of painting, then, this is not the black drawing that cuts into colour to inscribe its figures and landscapes, but colour that cuts into the blackness of the night, making images flower in its surrounding shadows.

The fact that neon lights are limited to the straightforward representation of luminous contours is explained primarily by technical reasons. It is almost impossible to manufacture neon lights whose volume does not follow the straightforward line but spreads out width-wise. The gas needs a relatively confined and length-wise space to be able to deliver all its potential phosphorescence. On the other hand the width denied in physical terms comes about through the power of diffusion of fluorescent light: confined in its glass tube, it creates halos which extend beyond its material bounds and which spread out *indefinitely* over the world around it. The lights are reflected across all the reflective surfaces in the city: shop windows, car bodywork, asphalt and wet roadways. It is not just artificial light's quite straightforward parodying of daylight; neon reinforces this mimicry by imitating one striking element of natural light: lightning flashes. As quick and fierce as lightning bolts, neon lights tear at the dark sky of the city as if to point out its fragility, attracting attention by their strangeness. Their sudden winking makes them seem aggressive and persistent, and their even frequency makes them seem reassuring and soothing. Their flashes disturb, while their repetition reassures.

Perhaps we haven't given enough emphasis so far to the fact that the most important aspect of a neon tube is precisely its winking. Quite unlike the light of day, which is constant and uniform for all its variations and shadings, neon light at once displays its artificial character through its on–off brilliance. The winking is not just designed to draw attention through the discontinuity it creates in the field of vision, it is in itself an indication of its own unnatural origin. The play of rhythms that arise from the winking as it goes on and on present almost endlessly possible combinations: sequencing, intersection, movement back and forth, etc. Neon therefore does not just offer the sight of its pure phosphorescence, enthralling though it may be, but it sets up sequences, rhythms and tempos. Like the natural elements which, by day, afford us a normal sense of direction and intuitive ordering of space, it articulates nocturnal life and gives it its bearings.

However, if we look at it from too close up or stare at it too long, the showy brightness of the neon lights is blinding. This is itself the paradox of the light that illuminates people and things sideways, but blinds those who want to look at it face on. Neon does not emerge from this contradiction, instead driving it to its paroxysm. It does not directly annihilate darkness, but rather gives it a monochrome tint. The night becomes blue, green, fuchsia. It is impossible not to reflect that, in the midst of its prolonged baths of colour where everything from night walkers to buildings is given the same hue, the sordid details and the *chiaroscuro* of the soul remain crouched in a shadow which physically no longer exists, but for all that goes on living under a different aspect.

Alas, the neon signs are progressively giving way to the walls of digital images. The medium of television is supplanting the archaic two-tone winking. It now clothes the city in a phoney complexity which makes one miss the naïve images and graphics of the signs that are fast disappearing.

In the face of such electrical debauchery, one enjoys imagining a sudden and total blackout which would plunge the world of the city into an endless night, like the one that paralysed New York for several hours in 1966, leaving people stuck in elevators, underground car parks and the subway, without any assistance or explanation. It would be interesting to see how organizations accustomed to the intense glare of the desert and the brightly lit nights would react in total darkness. But we can suppose that the energy produced in such profusion by Las Vegas is so great that, even in such an eventuality, the formidable electrical potency accumulated day after day inside buildings and people, preserved in bodies and minds, deposited upon skin and stone, would be enough on its own to get the town back on its feet again without anyone having noticed a thing.

Mass Ornament

Siegfried Kracauer's articles on the leisure industry in the *Frankfurter Zeitung*, published in the late 1920s, have given us an insight into how 'mass ornament', the fundamental structural element in this new society of leisure, combines an extreme rationality of means and an absurdity of ends. The ornamentation of advertising or spectacle, art or politics, architecture or sport, turns the mechanical process of society into a glamorous display of finery, a meaningless decorative flourish in which the *socius* can admire himself in the unique moment of a formal, all-embracing representation. The legs of the Tiller Girls, along with other new urban attractions (large-screen cinemas, gaming rooms, etc.) show off the creative power of the social process expunged of any human purpose. *Hic Rhodus, hic saltus.*

But the fact is that in Las Vegas the formative force of the process is no longer the mass itself in the candid virginity of its physical strength. It has been replaced by the mindless *déclassé* hordes that hang about shopping malls and amusement parks. The smooth, homogeneous cream of humanity that spreads everywhere like a protective balm has its origins in the universal middle class, wherever it may come from and whatever its native tongue. It has as its common dominator a certain inverted image of childhood, since, being incapable of altering a single iota of its mediocre reality, it has fixed itself upon acting out a great social regression into infantilism. Disinclined towards innocence, it has immediately abandoned any spirit of seriousness, which in its eyes is something embodied by critical minds, who are always splitting hairs about reality with their

sempiternal warnings, and has opened itself up compulsively to the regressive pleasures of hypo-cultural pee and shit. It has exiled itself from the ordinary world represented by political and social life and has found a cosy refuge in the magical and necessarily simple-minded memories of its very early life, when reality was sweetened and had none of the harshness that causes it to suffer so terribly. For it, Pinocchio's Playland no longer means a far-off place that can only be reached by chance (it has even forgotten that in the end the merrymakers are turned into donkeys), but a branch of Hollywood and Disney which has set itself up in the Mojave Desert to be crammed full of junk that spills out all over the place.

But in the translucent arteries of Las Vegas, the pomp of the means devoted to a ludic satisfaction is there only to mask the signal baseness of the depths and to cretinise the customer. Decoration has overtaken fundamentals, or rather it has managed to draw from shallowness itself its rarest essence: small-mindedness. At this advanced hour of the night, sometimes one takes to thinking that backward movement will soon reach its final phase and get stuck in the nullity of lost time. But there are still quantities of infinitesimal trivia around, and the stupidity displayed will always have scope for an even lower level that can be explored and exploited. Futility is bottomless. 'How much further are they going to go?', the man next to me asks, stunned by the explosion of light and sound from the Bellagio water fountain. It strikes me that the question doesn't have a negative ring to it.

Translating the Theme

What are the explanations for the fashion for theming in the entertainment industry of Las Vegas? We cannot regard as meaningful the trend towards the perfect imitation and the aim of reliving some period in history (Caesars Palace, The Luxor, The Excalibur) or experiencing the atmosphere of some original place (Paris, Treasure Island, Circus Circus), since the re-creations on offer are hardly convincing, even for a guy from Iowa. The argument so frequently advanced, and so dubious, that Americans are ignorant of history, is not viable. They are not dupes of their deliberate ignorance, nor do they make use of Las Vegas as a history book, in their notion of having a good time. What is more, all the casino hotels which present these historical or geographical reconstructions very often allow the interior of the building itself to contain heterogeneous architectural elements that stand in the way of any plausible acceptance. The Excalibur's fairytale castle, inspired by the palace of Neuschwanstein in Bavaria, rises up in the midst of a tropical lagoon. Inside the black pyramid of The Luxor nestle facades reminiscent of a Florentine palazzo.

The logic guiding the commercial strategy of a themed hotel or restaurant is more to do with the habitual experience of a film viewer. The cinema does indeed represent the major source of inspiration of the Las Vegas architecture and entertainments. At a show the audience is involved at the level of *what if*, being quite aware of the unreal nature of the staging and stifling any urge to verify the information supplied on stage. With an unrepentant lack of realism, the thematic element thus serves to endow a locale with the atmospheric unity of a film, with some

73

sense of its narrative components. What is more, the theming doesn't just enable some immediate recognition of its central subject, but also a play of variations which gives the customer the impression of an experience which in itself is rich and diverse. It hardly matters if some of the details are at odds with the end result, that the Julius Caesar looks like a cowboy or the towers of the castle bring to mind those of an international airport rather than a feudal fortress, the important thing resides in the repeated cadences of an essential idea which functions as a conduit for a whole range of activities, like some Ariadne's clue in the chaotic space of the city. Reassured by the unity and coherence of the different services on offer, the customer is then gladly disposed to consume, and, as with a children's fairytale, wants to keep on being told the same story.

From the Sublime to the Grotesque

Without the least uncertainty, Las Vegas has set its just measure in excess, its happy medium in extremes. Nothing in the city can be promoted unless it is susceptible to infinite exaggeration. The mafioso Sodom of Bugsy Siegel, Meyer Lansky and the Teamsters Union underwent a metamorphosis into an urban Disneyland for families in the early 1980s, when gambling was legalized in other States of the Union, and Nevada's monopoly thereby came to an end. But whether it's with a passion for gambling or theme park worship, liberation through endless consumption, of personal and financial resources, remains just the same.

Las Vegas goes in for out and out excess, and yet there is nothing that you could really call sublime. Here, the grandiose turns into the grotesque, and the exaggeration of proportions only gives way to an extreme desire to laugh. At first sight one might have thought that the colossal signs or the gigantic hotels that line the Strip would arouse in the spectator a feeling of space opening out and a terror of collapse. But this is not the case. In fact, as Burke and Kant had seen in the late eighteenth century, the experience of the sublime entails the impossibility of comparing the size of one's own body to the almost infinite grandeur in the face of which it is robbed of any canonical value. But the monumental aspect of the various casinos and attractions in Las Vegas does not refer in any way to our own bodies as possible standards of comparison. It has nothing to do with us. This is its sense of the grotesque: the grandiose devoid of interest.

Even though the architecture of Las Vegas is imposing,

perhaps more striking in its size and strictly visual effects than the major works of humankind, like the pyramids of Egypt or the Aztec temples, we cannot say that the feeling we have when we see it has anything to do with experiencing respect or awe before its monumentality. The excess that characterizes Las Vegas is not a matter of infinite grandeur but of mere comic emphasis. The spatial and sensory disproportion that transports us abruptly from one extreme to another, for example from the dark interior of the casinos to the exterior brightness of the desert, far from leading to an experience of astonishment that is a mixture of the disturbing and the exciting, comes down to nothing more in the end than straightforward architectural self-promotion.

Opening and Closing

'Probably no place else in the history of modern city building was developed on a single idea the way Las Vegas was. The closest thing to it is Hollywood, which grew by exporting its idea, but the Vegas idea can't leave town. It has nothing for export but its promise. Its growth was not only conspicuous, conspicuousness was the only medium of its growth.'
Michael Herr
The Big Room (1986)

The old Downtown casinos (The Golden Nugget, The Glitter Gulch, etc.), like the very first hotel complexes built further south on the Strip (The Sands, The Desert Inn, etc.), resembled mournful windowless hospitals, charmless blocks of concrete. When the lights on the signs went out at daybreak they gave way to a crude and shabby architecture of featureless grey rectangles looming behind the cacti in the distance. Stripped of their neon embellishments, the casinos were no more than warehouses devoid of visual interest. But gradually, in the early 1970s, what the architects Venturi, Scott Brown and Izenour called the 'decorated shed'[9] (where the symbolic components covered the exterior of the architectural form without profoundly altering it) was transformed into a 'duck', and the outward structure became both symbol and self-reference. Tired of its intrinsic lack of appeal, the building then reappropriated into its internal form the symbolic content which previously had been exiled to the signs and posters.

The declared aim of the various promoters of the themed casinos, like Steve Wynn or Jay Sarno, was to compete on equal terms with Hollywood, by offering to a public constantly in search of novelty a free, live show in the open air. To attract passers-by to the gambling halls, they had the idea of opening up the casino onto the street and transferring the show from the big entertainment hall where it usually took place out onto the city pavements. From then on the building turned into a visual magnet, a representation. It put itself on stage.

This meant that at any hour of the day or night, without any need for tickets or reservations, you could watch a pirate attack on a galleon, see medieval jousting, or a chase through the streets of New York. By opening out the shows from the halls and the parks, the Las Vegas promoters created the street show, the city as mass medium. In this new extravagant and spend-thrift space, they combined techniques of cinematography, set design and painting to fashion a place totally devoted to enter-tainment.

But this largesse had a price. The opening towards outside only has a point if it makes it concomitantly easier to shut the spectators inside the building's anonymous interior. The extravagance and the free entry to attractions, indeed some-times even complimentary hotel services (drinks, a buffet, cut-price rooms), has no other aim but to lead all comers to invest in the only activity which always recoups its stake: gambling. In other words, the architectural and playful generosity of Las Vegas is only equalled by its worth as a lure for gain.

A.C.

The conditioned air that pours like icy fluid out of the huge air-conditioning units in every building in Las Vegas has the strange faculty of making us believe in our own declimatization from the world around us.

Cut off from the world by a film of atmosphere, we look on, watching everything in its very act of retreating, bereaved of all proximity. We are cryogenized while still alive, like babies in a cellophane bubble trying their utmost to renew lost contact with reality. It seems to us that we are moving forward on a permanent air-cushion, swimming effortlessly in an undefinable atmosphere that annihilates all sensation of weight and resistance. With neither bodies nor presence, we float along the pathways like ghosts, the few tiny drops of sweat shyly intimated on our brow being instantly turned into crystals of ice, thereby showing us that our process of mineralization is underway.

Beyond Beauty and Ugliness

It would be out of place to imagine that Las Vegas represents the pinnacle of bad taste. Contrary to received opinion, it is no more than commonplace. Not that it cultivates any sense of distinction or tact. One need only visit the Liberace Museum for a formal denial of any aesthetic intentions on the part of the city. Las Vegas has long since left behind the stage of good taste, or more precisely of culture in general. By virtue of its capacity for universal appeal, it has absorbed every artistic, cultural and social value (for example its parodic recuperation of the institution of marriage) into the bottomless pit of its excess, and has made it all in a certain way innocent and puerile, dull and indifferent. Las Vegas is a pretend city, a city without pretensions. Snapping its fingers at any seriousness of thought, it merely wants to have a good time without any regrets, to consume itself in good clean fun and the frenzy of all and sundry.

As Nathanael West wrote in *The Day of the Locust*, of Hollywood in the 1930s, that open-air Hollywood for the middle classes: 'It is hard to to laugh at the need for beauty and romance, no matter how tasteless, even horrible, the results of that are. But it is easy to sigh. Few things are sadder than the truly monstrous.'[10] And these observations are equally valid for Las Vegas *a fortiori*.

So, for Las Vegas the issue of cultural distinction doesn't even exist. It has invented a way of life that can do without any recourse to some past experience as the basis for cultural transmission and as a reference for valuing the present. Its devotion (for it is capable of veneration) goes to straightforward 'immediate gratification', as Joan Didion put it. It wallows in the moment, and it couldn't care less about links with tradition or looking to the future. It lives from day to day, without any concern for what it would like to be or to have been. If all its principal buildings were to be transformed wholesale into something else tomorrow, it would take no notice, nor would it see any harm in it. Wearing new clothes, it would give itself up all over again to its irrepressible passion: frivolous extravagance. When it imitates New York or Paris, as in two of its recent productions of graphic architecture, this is not out of any nostalgia or desire to be a city. This is simply a testimony to its power of assimilating that worldwide urbanity which it ingests like everything else without actually digesting it or being nourished. It is a city without shame that swallows up other cities to the point of reappropriating their urban icons, in its own style, and supplanting them as a tourist destination.

The true power of Las Vegas lies in what one might call its 'blessed ignorance'. Sin City now commits only sins of omission; it has forgotten the very reasons for its being reprehensible. The key to its inner workings is in fact to be found in its deep-rooted unknowingness, its way of not taking any umbrage over its lack of knowledge, but in playing with this and enjoying it. None the less this deliberate ignorance demands a constant impetus and daily maintenance. Likewise it cannot entirely detach itself from all culture and strip bare the foundations of Western civilization without some practical skills, some kind of aptitude for taking people in; and likewise it cannot palm off such a jumble of make-believe without any real symbolic substance on a man of good sense who is not all that easily duped, without some talent for illusionism. If we could manage at all to forge a synthetic image of Las Vegas and its multiple facets, we should not be that far from discovering, in this potency of playful commercial conviction, the solution to its enigma as a city. Behind the bric-à-brac of make-believe, which at first sight raises a smile, is concealed probably the most formidable social armada of all time, combining, in one place, commercial seductiveness and technological appeal.

American Dream

'Las Vegas is one of the most generous towns in the world.'
Jeremy Railton
producer, Fremont Street Experience light show

In this non-stop flood of popular icons whose aim is to exhaust
the present so as to give it some consistency, there is none the
less one thing that remains strangely invisible in Las Vegas. Yet
it is at the very bedrock of the city: money. Strictly speaking,
only its sign is to be seen, but never its colour. The sign is everywhere, hugely displayed on the facades of the casinos and
printed on T-shirts. It serves as decoration for the halls, as a
template for shapes, as a motif on menu headings. It is gambled
with, it is lived off, and yet it holds itself back, forever inacces-
sible. *Deus absconditus*. By hook or by crook, the Las Vegas
promoters set out to make it disappear as an object. It is their
concerted purpose to make the customer forget the very idea of
money. Cash has to be disposed of, so that you don't have to
worry about it any more. In order to spend it, one has to act as if
it no longer had any value. Devalued, its only use is in the play
of signs: the chips you exchange it for on the way into the
casinos. Without any tangible substance, it can thus circulate
more efficiently, move about with ease and fluidity. It can obliterate its symbolic value the better to take on its market value.
Making the gambler believe that money doesn't matter, that it's
not what is important, that what counts most of all is having a
good time. This is the trick used by the various gambling
promoters, so there can be no question of them paying the
slightest attention to the price of things. Instead, they aim to

short-circuit all monetary reckonings, to obliterate the value of everything. This is the reason why, over and over, they promote a general atmosphere of things being free of charge. In this universe without the reality of cost, average consumers who keep their budget in mind feel as if they have fallen into a horn of plenty. Everything strikes them as being generously given.

But what does Las Vegas get out of it? What does it really have to offer us? For, in this phantasmagorical fairground which challenges the imagining of figures by its excess, and that of letters by default, the gambling businesses give away no product or merchandise. Their liberality lies elsewhere. They give something you can see, but nothing you can own. Both literally and figuratively, you always leave Las Vegas with empty pockets. There is nothing to buy, apart from a few post-cards or cheap T-shirts that you could buy anywhere else. Unlike the world fairs of the nineteenth century which presented themselves as great collective bazaars, as complete exhibitions of worldwide goods and merchandise, the casino hotels exhibit nothing, unless it is their technological artillery of lures and artifices.

The only thing offered to the customers, and still without all the advertising they would have a right to expect, is money, or to be more precise the idea of money, which is to say the fact of being able to win it easily by gambling. This is a peculiar economic mechanism: money is promised to those whom one moreover incites to get rid of it without further ado. Less is more. You always need to touch rock bottom before you can get your hands on the big prize. In gambling there is no other moral: sink low and put your hopes on coming out a winner at the end. However, that's not what matters and the gambler is no fool.

The casinos offer something quite different from the mere lure of winning: they give you a dream. This is all just make-believe and projection. But to what end? For the sake of what reality? What, for instance, is the ultimate purpose of the scene-setting from antiquity at Caesars Palace? It is certainly not to educate the onlooker about social and political conditions in ancient Rome. The reference to a historical or fictional theme is enough in itself. It prompts no exegesis, just confining itself to allusion that is part irony, part fabulation. Given that its existence is solely a commercial one, what is it then that Las Vegas produces and sells?

The only article it trades in is the power to participate on a modest scale in the show; to walk alongside the legionaries and the vestals, to act as *if you were there*. The one and only market value is therefore represented by the consumers' own imagination. They unwittingly bring with them the instrument of their own bad luck. It is they who turn the shows into a party, who feed the urban monster with their own energy, day after day. Las Vegas would not have been possible if the consumer society had not already been exploiting all of the ludic resources of popular fables, mainstream cinema and light fiction since the start of the twentieth century. It is this low-level culture which gives it a semblance of life, which fills out the empty forms of its cut-price symbolism.

As a result, the crowds come to contribute to the electric orgy so that they may glimpse their dreams being given substance for the space of a moment (are they really their dreams anyway?) or just their ordinary fads. They spend recklessly not in the hope that in the end they will win (they are not that naïve when it comes to their regular work), but to buy now, and for a few all too short moments, that which has no price: make-believe, visions and dreams (the kitsch imagery of the casinos fulfilling this imaginary function of transporting them to a world of make-believe).

When all is said and done, make-believe, in its multifarious embodiments, is the only merchandise for which Americans are capable of ruining themselves with no one standing in their way. The American dream does not mean, as is too often believed, that every dream can at any moment come true, can turn from rags to riches, but much rather that the only conscious reality in America is the very fact of dreaming. The American dream is to enable each American citizen, whoever he or she may be, to have the power simply to dream. For them, dreaming almost has the status of a self-fulfilling prophecy, in the sense that the mere fact of dreaming already constitutes the dream, which is another way of describing the success of the ideology of fantasy.

Through its ethos of self-reliance, which was inspired by Emerson and gradually became muddied into the perfunctory psychology of the winner, America has inculcated into its populace not the dream of success, but the one and only success of the dream. Because dreaming already means having won. Deep down everyone knows this, the dream long glimpsed by everyone will only really come true for some, and worse still for those who perhaps deserve it the least; but every individual, be they winner or loser, already has within them *the reality of the dream*.

In the everyday daydream of material success and happiness, dreaming is enough in itself. Likewise, measured by this yardstick, half-realities are worth more than some solid reality laid down for once and all. By this token, it is not those who fail who are disappointed, since the possibility of a new dream is still there, always present and available, and with it success at the end of the road, but those who, whether through failure or success, have lost even the faculty to dream: the pessimist, the killjoy, the nostalgic. Even people who live at the bottom of the social scale, and who will not see even the slightest hint of their various social fantasies, are proud of their dreams. These mean more to them than anything else. To have them taken away in their eyes represents a real social crime, an assault on their dignity. Beaten down and humiliated, in some recess of their being they always have a cut-price fantasy to hand: a villa in California, a Pontiac convertible, a trip to Hawaii, even a more down-to-earth pair of Levi jeans, or a voucher for a free meal at Hardee's. Their real wealth is merely the idea of wealth.

From this perspective, I espouse the views of Jonathan Raban, who observes, in *Hunting Mister Heartbreak*, that:

> *Dream* was the codeword for that ache for transcendence, for moving up and moving on, which had been sanctioned by the republic as a democratic right. As the grave voice-over in a TV ad for an investment company put it, 'Because Americans want to *succeed*, not just survive . . .' Success here didn't merely mean moving from position A to a more comfortable berth at B; it was, rather, a quality endemic to your personality and your national character – a peculiarly American state of being, in which you were continuously aspiring, striving, becoming. To dream was to keep faith with the idea that there was always a new frontier, a storey at least one floor above that on which you were now living. It was an authenticating mark of the true-hearted American.[11]

Conversely, anti-Americans are those who are unwilling to play the game of collective self-deception, and refuse to dream their reality or, more accurately, to live according to their dreams. They are those who deny not just the eventual possibility of succeeding, but most of all the possibility of the possibility of succeeding. People for whom a dream of some unilateral success is already a sign of social failure or of the shameless exploitation of credulity.

We can easily laugh at the average American, regard him as a big kid or an appalling ignoramus, but we cannot rob him of that which all the Continental political philosophers hope for – if we read between the lines – from the silent populations to whom they address their works of social reform: that they sacrifice everything for the sake of their dream, however paltry it may be. The collective utopia of the United States is made manifest, so to speak, in the sum total of the personal utopias whose spatial projection lies at the heart of the Nevada Desert.

Googie Style

'The city, however, does not tell its past, but contains it like the lines of a hand, written in the corners of the streets, the gratings of the windows, the banisters of the steps, the antennae of the lightning rods, the poles of the flags, every segment marked in turn with scratches, indentations, scrolls.'

Italo Calvino
Invisible Cities

Most of the signs and buildings put up in the 1950s and '60s in Las Vegas are in the style known as googie, a kind of syncretism between Art Nouveau and the comic strip, futurism and cartoons. The electric flower on the Drink and Eat Too bar is a perfect illustration of this. Here you see the same eclectic fondness for coiling tendrils of vegetation, organic curves and zoomorphic arabesques, science-fiction decor and the moulded-plastic cocktail lounge, but seen through the distorting prism of primary colours and crude comic-book effects. Something fizzy and unpolished, primitive and good-natured. This exaggeration and simplification endows its works with a humorous touch which Guimard's Paris Métro entrances certainly do not possess. It has all gone through the mill of excess and saturation, producing an 'effect of everything blending together' which, for the critic Roger de Piles, was the definition *par excellence* of Baroque art. With its pop-luxurious appearance of a pink-hued flying saucer with audacious angles and Hawaiian curves, the now defunct Mint belonged to this noble, part-primitive, part-visionary dynasty of the googie building. There seemed to be nothing keeping it on the ground. No impression of gravity emanated from its bio-technological form.

Another great source of inspiration for the designers of urban electricity derives from aircraft cabins and the customized bodywork of cars. The modern celebration of speed and propulsive force is to be found here on the Strip in such examples as the aggressive oblong forms of the awnings of diners or advertising billboards that literally slash the air. With the selfsame carefree exaltation, technology and nature seamlessly combine in the urban electrograph, seeking to create a continuum between all the different elements of the city (buildings, parks, automobiles). Leaves, clad in hard brightness, become like steel; cars and machines for their part assume the biomorphic appearance of a plant or flowering tree.

In general, the roadside components of commercial architecture now have little to do with what can be learned in a school of architecture, instead relating to the ordinary lived experience of the American citizen's working day, condensed into some synthetic form. The Googie style thus uses all the potential resources offered by the suburban visual universe: cars, movies, television, newspapers, advertising posters, comic strips, etc., and turns buildings into an extension of the cultural environment, without any concern for its integration into its natural setting. By their displacement from their usual context and by the no less surprising eclecticism of their composition, it metamorphoses these primitive forms into a puerile and unpretentious festival which is tasted like an ice cream before it melts. It is out of all this that a city is made: the relationship between forms and materials, images and quotations which interact within the limits of space and the bounds of time.

The Conspiracy of Chance

Because in a society in which the only currency is currency, and where most of us are absolutely irrelevant and power-less economic entities, to sit down at any Vegas table creates at least the illusion of empowerment.
Mark Cooper
Searching for Sin City and finding Disney in the Desert (1993)

The process whereby an ordinary day unfolds in Las Vegas has over decades been perfectly honed, down to the smallest details, and even the most surprising and exceptional events are no more than opportunities for verifying that the everyday mechanism is in good working order. Nonetheless, the entire system of gambling, for all its controls, rests upon what is in the end a relatively fragile base: chance. This is not a matter of the chance involved in gambling itself (everything is programmed by computer), but of the chance involved in human behaviour.

It must indeed require a good deal of recklessness to give up money hard earned, by inserting coin after coin in slot machines in the hope of winning more than your stake, just like so many others before you. So the only question that arises for every promoter comes down to this: how can this disturbing element of irrationality be eliminated from gambling? How can you bet on the gamblers who act without any reason to act as they do? For, on the one hand, the casino owners are also taking a gamble on the gamblers and on the other, in as much as a conscious being can be aware of it, every gambler *has the chips*.

In order to attenuate the gambler's dread of knowingly throwing away his or her money and losing it all in the end, the

promoters and other engineers create around them a whole context of distraction and reassurance. Everything is done to minimize the terror of loss. The colours in which the gambling halls are decorated are warm, the fabrics thick and quilted. At every point, any fear or feeling of panic must be eliminated, for they could overturn the whole edifice by paralysing the customers. Of course, the casinos live off the risk taken by the gamblers, but they cannot master every single component aspect, like, for example, the anxiety which could turn against them were it to change into resentment. In the risk itself, they seek constantly to separate the wheat (the bet) from the chaff (dread), and turn wild prodigality into a kind of festive *potlatch* where, against his long-term interest, the model punter sacrifices his monthly salary on the altar of gambling.

Nor should we despise the true intentions of the gambler, at the other end of the chain which makes up the world of gambling. Contrary to the commonly held idea that being better informed about the internal workings of the casino would make him stop wanting to gamble, the gambler well knows what he is doing. But for him gambling is not the issue. He does not bet in order to pick up the stake or carry off the prize. From his point of view winning does not really matter in the end. When he places his bet and throws the dice, it is so that, for the space of an all too brief moment that he wants endlessly to prolong, he can feel the troubling sense of pure possibility. As he waits for the outcome he is acutely alert to the experience of chance, the sudden frisson of *tuchè* falling from heaven and singling him out as the happy beneficiary among human beings. At heart, the gambler isn't wishing for any cash or cheque; he leaves that to the smug and the destitute. In his ludic drive, he wants something completely *immaterial*: the probable, the plausible, the uncertain. His quest could not be less venal. What he seeks is that propitious moment when the order of things meets the order of desires, when two sequences of events coincide in the right number being held in his hands. He wants to be that living crossroads between his own individual decision and the universal purposes of the cosmos.

In his frenetic intent to stuff coins one after the other into the slot machines, the gambler aspires thereby in a magic way to make concrete the obscure forces which govern the world, to render effective the making of a choice whose particulars are inscrutable to him. In one sense, all he seeks is the failure of his undertaking, which, more than its success, will give him the possibility of once more experiencing the pure possibility of winning, and so on and so forth repeated. Deep down, he feels bad about this progression *ad infinitum*. He would like the game never to stop, and for that to happen he must not only accept losing, but aspire to lose. In his heart of hearts he knows very well that winning would put an end to the game, just as fulfilment completes a desire. When he immediately places his bet again, it is because he regards his winnings, however big they are, as not yet being an expression of success.

Background Noise

The cacophony of manufactured entertainment gradually fades to give way to a faint but continuous background noise, which then mingles with other city sounds that stand out as thinly distinct strata (the hum of traffic, planes taking off, the play of the wind in the branches) in a kind of layered crust of sound. Here, in aisle B 23 of a trailer park in the north-east suburbs of Las Vegas, Rico is doing his washing. He plunges his tattooed arms into the basin sitting on the dusty, insalubrious ground, and listlessly agitates an openwork coat of mail. He stops for a moment, dries his hands on the back of his denims and lights a cigarette. Behind him, on the steps of his breezeblock-mounted chalet, a woman watches him out of the corner of her eye, the way you would keep an eye on a child, then, her expression dull and mournful, she closes the screen door, so rickety it stays shut only with a fastening.

Here, in a neighbourhood where 'eat in or to go?' is routine, in a neighbourhood of cut-price existences, parking lots and Sundays where the family gets together in shopping malls, in a neighbourhood of lives stripped of any solid relation to the world and to other people, Rico gets ready for the fray. Too poor to protect himself against the lord, he placed himself in his service. Tonight he will sweat, wrestle and do battle, attached to a rope ten feet above the ground, overlooking the clients at the restaurant of the Excalibur, as they sit hunched over their plates.

Urban Monster or Future Normality?

The Strip's theme architecture makes it a video screen of the national consciousness.
Alan Hess
Viva Las Vegas

Under pain of missing its true essence, one should not regard Las Vegas as an anomaly. Over and above the weirdness of these architectural forms, it is a formidable construction site for future urban trends. Although in a sense it defies all categorization because of its extravagance and its protean nature, it nonetheless presents a means of studying *in situ* those post-industrial cities that, in the wake of the decline in manufacturing and industrial work, aim to organize themselves around the channels for mass service and leisure businesses.

As Alan Hess puts it, 'The Las Vegas Strip . . . is the ultimate version of the commercial strips found on the fringes of almost all American cities.'[12] Little by little each of these towns is beleaguered by the playful and secondary eclecticism of its design, in so far as it is subject to the same structural problems that have been encountered and resolved by the *capital of gambling*: the massive presence of cars, architecture as visitor attraction, the invasiveness of advertising. This is why the monstrous urban character of Las Vegas is all too apparent, for in the inner life of its own forms, 'Las Vegas was based on the innovations of the car culture and particularly the motel.'[13] Far from being a deformed exception in American town planning, it brilliantly synthesizes its every aspect, and prefigures all its directions to come. There is nothing so much resembling the city as this denial of the city.

If we are to grasp the meaning of these new peripheral cities, without any centre or precise boundary – 'Edge Cities', as Joel Garreau termed them – Las Vegas will be an extremely useful tool for understanding, since it has turned disorientation into a pattern for spatial and urban organization. In this sea of uniform concrete, it has let thematic and iconographic architectures flower and create enclaves of identification; spatial, but also temporal and commemorative landmarks. Nor is it surprising likewise to see these allegorical buildings grow in suburban spaces where all traditional geographical distinctions are blurred.

Besides, Las Vegas was built around the car and for it, thus becoming the first Roadtown in the land. It has even exported the model of the Strip as an expression of successful integration within a linear perspective of diverse urban functions (motels, leisure spaces, casinos, wedding chapels, supermarkets). All the major problems of American suburbia (traffic flow and direction, ease of access to buildings by the roadway, etc) have been raised, thought about and to a certain degree surmounted. 'A roadway could become a city. A building could become a sign. In no place at all, someplace could be created. This is the genius of Las Vegas.'[14]

All the same, one need not feel compelled to espouse the optimism of Alan Hess, who sees in the human interactions of a casino hall an acceptable model for social intercourse, one that would replace the now obsolete interactions of old urban relationships.

In a casino the social interaction is focused on entertainment. If the model is applied to developing Edge Cities, it could adapt to social and political functions as well.[15]

This is a frightening prospect. As we have seen, this is precisely the Las Vegas utopia of having us believe that it is a city and that, as a city, it can provide a comfortable urban life.

In Hess's defence, however, it is true that the whole of the citiness of Las Vegas is in its every innermost recess dictated by motives of consumerism and that these, despite their total glorification of the one and only consumerist monad, have succeeded in creating embryonic forms of interpersonal relations, a semblance of urban life which in its turn influences the other urban spaces which are not exclusively connected to the unique power of buying and selling.

Echoing the admonitions of Lewis Mumford or Joan Didion, we can certainly deplore the fact that the creative power of the contemporary urban landscape, in roadside architecture and advertising design, is essentially commercial. Nevertheless we must not forget that the old constitutive forces of the city (Church and State) pursued no less coercive ends in their slow strategy of planning the cities of the world. Unlike those two former candidates, the consumer society does not seek to establish itself in time, nor even to transform its durability into authority. It thrives on the basis of instantaneous presence, and repeatable impulsiveness. To some degree, its continual everyday injunctions (advertising, strategies for appealing to customers, etc.), though artistically camouflaged as benevolent enticements, are more pressing and aggressive than the political and religious demands which occupy the public stage.

All the same, its nature is not at issue. It is connected to the very mode of functioning of a market society. Because it knows that it is fundamentally much more fragile than the order of the sacred or the State, its masks this weakness beneath a much exaggerated pugnacity. Since it does not demand in addition the individual's total giving of self or absolute identification with its model, in the way that the Church or the State could demand these of the faithful or of citizens, it must thereupon extract all that it can from the customer's present wish, for it is betting definitively on something extremely versatile: covetousness.

This is the reason why the vernacular architecture of mass consumerism quite consciously neglects the building for the sake of its allegorical appearance, disregarding the thesis for the sake of the theme, foundation for the sake of ostentation. It does not seek to endure, to set down roots, but to sell things there and then. Moreover its spatial character proper is swallowed up by the temporality of the instant, the sudden moment of conversion to purchasing. Unlike courts of justice and cathedrals, the constructions of routine architecture, of which Las Vegas, along with Los Angeles, is probably the capital, deliberately renounce any effect of durability, for their aim is not membership, confidence in institutions or belief in dogmas, just the instantaneous attraction that will lead to the no less impetuous action of a volatile desire for possession.

Anything Goes

Thirty million visitors in the year 2000; an annual turnover of 4.3 thousand million dollars; 10 casino hotels that have each cost more than 500 million dollars and offer an average of 3,000 rooms. The list of edifying figures gets longer, and it serves as live publicity for the city. In Las Vegas numbers have definitively replaced letters. The overall sway of abbreviations bears witness to it: the city has sacrificed its own name and calls itself just Vegas. But behind this victory of numbers over letters, we must also equally note the no less conquering privilege of universal equivalence. In Analphabet City everything counts, from the cents with their own slot machine at the Glitter Gulch or the Horseshoe, to the thousands of millions plastered all over the city. The logic of number implies that everything has some kind of equal value, so long as it is easily quantifiable. Instead of creating difference and grandeur, it brings each and every figure, no matter how huge, down to a straightforward adding up of identical units.

As a result all the extravagances offered by Las Vegas in its theme parks and mass entertainments have the shared feature of having the potential for at least being numerically compatible. It doesn't matter what people choose to do there. Anything at all will bring the money in. This is the new teaching of Las Vegas: 'whatever you do, do it.' For Michael Ventura it is the embodiment of the city of Anything:

> We loved Las Vegas because we knew the house rules, which are as follows: as long as you don't bother the other customers, you can do *anything*.
> That's the promise of Vegas: Anything.[16]

Here, the pursuit of happiness, written into the U.S. Constitution as a Federal right, attains its final goal: unrestricted enjoyment, at any price, in any way and with anyone, but enjoyment all the same. This programmed insouciance, however, conceals a less rosy reality.

We find that, in his piece of reportage, Michael Ventura offers a terrifying image of the city of gambling: a high suicide rate among the young, tourists who freak out and get the shakes after gambling for too long without eating, Mexican and Native American populations dumped far out of town . . . As we follow him on the trail of this strangeness that is taken for granted, deep inside this 'mall of anything', we become keenly aware of the plastic and protean nature of contemporary capitalism, which is always ready to change its skin so that it doesn't lose out. Everything can be bought and sold, and Las Vegas itself deals in what, strictly speaking, doesn't exist. For this is why, as Ventura has clearly perceived, it accommodates to everything, bends to all desires, fulfils all demands, however cranky, like those of the psychotic millionaires who took up residence there (Howard Hughes, Stupak), so long as they don't disturb the next guy out of his daze. *Anything* has always been its habitual way of being, even in the days of the Mormons and the bandits.[17] And there is no limit to this canvassing without an object.

On the wall of one of the new giant casinos being built in the early 1990s, Ventura discovered a piece of graffiti, something rare in this town which is purged of all urban life, and in his view summing up the whole situation of Las Vegas and the hyper-capitalist spirit that guides it: One Step Beyond.

Six years later, encouraged by this revelation, I went in search of the inscription. I knew deep down, of course, that I had no likelihood of unearthing it, given the size and the constantly changing nature of the city. But it seemed to me that I ought not to renounce my task for all that; the reason was the attachment I had (even though I was unswervingly convinced of its absurdity) to that simple prophecy as the direct effect of the surrounding *anything*. I saw my tenacity as having the value of a homage to the city of happy irrationality. After two or three days of getting nowhere, wandering around the city and its outskirts, in a street parallel to Fremont Street, on a wall adjoining the Golden Nugget parking lot, I came across the sought-after magic words on the wall. This was not Ventura's inscription, but it went much further than what I had been expecting. As if to revenge itself for the bad thoughts I had come up with about it, in its great magnanimity the city had granted my wishes. It had not held my critical remarks against me, probably viewing them, rightly, as a harmless attack. So I don't know whether it was my naïve hope that had managed to write these words in advance (nothing is impossible in Las Vegas, where the mind can move mountains) or whether someone reading my thoughts, perhaps at a gambling table, had set out to fulfil my quest, but I then read, with unconcealed pleasure, inscribed in red letters on the white-brick wall: *Anything Goes.*

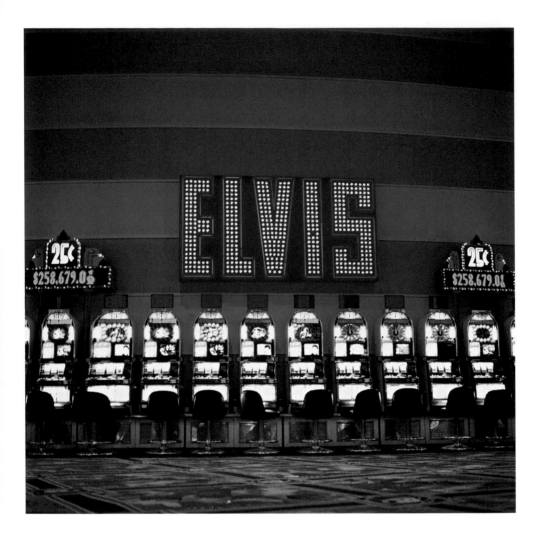

Leaving Las Vegas

It would be totally simplistic to imagine that the city of Las Vegas could coincide with what we can see of it or say about it. Since the power of its unreality derives precisely from the nature of its atmosphere, allowing no scope for capturing it either corporeally or intellectually, we are compelled to abandon any attempt at synthesizing it. Las Vegas makes sure to provoke in all those who experience it, whether at a mental or physical level, what one might call a disorder of representations, this being a confusion so intensely lived that it stands in the way of us reaching any identification with something that we can know or recognise.

Yet, in this swirl of images and sensations that are both extreme and volatile, one character trait remains forever visible: its Manichaeism. It is certainly not my intention to talk about its propensity to understand everything in terms of either good or evil (on the contrary, we have seen that it is placed beyond the classic transcendentals of truth, beauty and goodness), but its tendency constantly to interpret reality according to a crudely dualist classification. The victory of Las Vegas over our tastes and our feelings, even over the sweep of our aesthetic and political judgments, lies in having been able to impose an antagonistic doctrine of values. Its basic point of view sees everything that can be the object of human appreciation as reduced to the final and incontestable categories of the tedious and the entertaining, of what is boring and what is fun. There is no other possible option: either the dreariness of daily life or the magic of this town. From the point when you agree to enter into its binary *Weltanschauung*, everything in existence, be it real or merely ideal, comes down to this simplistic bipolarity which, by dint of repeated slogans and spectacular attractions, dominates all grasp of reality and inevitably crushes all other degrees of sensibility and inclination between its two extremes.

The monotony of this never-ending city actually lends itself to the alternating quality of its particular urban experience. Out of nowhere, the monotony gives way to unchecked eruptions of novelties that clash and shock within this fundamentally undifferentiated setting. Like those desert flowers that compensate for the aridity of their environment with an explosion of shapes and colours, as if everything continuing to live despite it had been gathered and condensed in them in paroxysmal guise, its urban architecture counterbalances the material poverty of the city with a boundless visual and expressive profusion of forms: eccentric buildings, giant signs, streamers bearing information, logos of every kind, etc. On the one hand the society of mass consumption has slowly impoverished daily life to the point of reducing it to a skeleton (the satisfaction of vital needs), while on the other it has, no less continually, reintroduced a semblance of life, flesh and attributes under the appearance of the phantasmagoria of advertising and play. Thus, like communicating vessels, everyday life and its Las Vegas transfiguration exchange their simplification and their false depth.

In Las Vegas there is only one rung on the ladder of pleasures: fun. All other possible kinds of contentment, not to say happiness, are systematically ignored or, even worse, put through the mincer of total entertainment, and those that cannot be turned into playthings for mechanical mirth are banished forever from its domain, stigmatized as dismal, humdrum and insignificant. All laughter is alike, all gratification sports the same device: entertainment. Las Vegas blows hot and cold, with nothing in between. There is no alternative to its vision of things: every single thing must either be in line with the puerile phantasmagoria or be rejected for once and all and be indelibly labelled as dull.

For example, the themed restaurants in the huge casinos twist the straightforward pleasure of enjoying a good wine or appreciating a dish into the all-embracing entertainment of a picturesque and invasive decor, with waiters in costume acting a part or noisy antics between the tables, as if, when all was said and done, the satisfaction of food and drink was not enough in itself but had to be accompanied straight away by a froth of architecture and noise to get the most out of it. Everything in Las Vegas that aspires to enjoyment, whether it is to do with need or desire, with the organic or the human, in some way takes on the exaggerated form of total entertainment. Between the two extremes of humdrum and fun, elected as the very principles of all judgement, nothing else can survive. Each state of awareness is irreversibly drawn, like a frail barque, into one of these two yawning abysses. So, in this city of Nevada, day and night, the law of the radical alternative governs every possibility of existence. With neither pause nor transition, life swings between the ordinary and the spectacular, from the *next to nothing* (what you have) to the *more than everything* (what you could imagine), leaving all and sundry with the notion that no other possible way of being can exist outside these dichotomous modes. More than any words or images, it is this denial of the infinite shades of sorrow and of pleasure, this aesthetic purging of our inclinations, that marks Vegas life.

This is why in Las Vegas entertainment undergoes a profound change in character. It is not a matter of it lifting us away from the reality around us into some imaginary experience, be it consolatory or critical, in accordance with the two great modes of the fictional imagination. Escapism no longer plays its part here. In the traditional theory of the role of entertainment, it should in fact assume the function of relieving the rigours of everyday life, particularly those of hard toil. Born of the separation from the world of seriousness, leisure offers respite in the relaxation and distraction necessary for a renewal of strength. Whether it be pure relief or an aspiration to some kind of self-creation, entertainment always sets itself in direct opposition to the world of work, to which it offers competing forms (even though Adorno and Horkheimer have very rightly shown how the leisure industry, while aiming to offer spectacles which seemingly deny work, has as its purpose the legitimation and reinforcement of it). In this sense, the world of leisure, whether stupefying or critical, always sees itself as taking its distance from the serious realm of everyday reality. But in Las Vegas entertainment no longer stands for one cultural component among others, even if it is a profound departure from our conception of what ought to be listed under the heading of cultural activity, instead it tends to incorporate the whole of culture and thereby to extend its grip on human reality. The boundary between the serious and the amusing, the everyday and the recreational, becomes muddled here. Not only does leisure in the Vegas fashion absorb every single cultural form (literature, the theatre, the plastic arts, philosophical ideas), but it tends equally to remodel everything that is part and parcel of civilization. The analysis given by Adorno and Horkheimer in their famous article 'The Culture Industry: Enlightenment as Mass Deception' needs some revision here: the culture industry does not just aspire to control over all the manifestations of culture, whose forms and basis it distorts through a simplifying standardization, it goes much further than this mere domination over the sphere of leisure. It now attempts to impose entertainment as the one and only rule of all human activity, be it work or play, quotidian or cultural. It now aims to be civilization, not culture; to be the total mode of production of a society rather than its refined form of self-understanding.

Thus we are witnessing the decompartmentalization of the industry of the spectacle, which, on the strength of its victories in the realm of leisure, now aims to carry out its wholesale assault on all areas of human life, particularly those of work and consumption. It is no longer a matter of the culture

industry softening the evils of industrial society, nor even justi-
fying them (an operation that has long since already been
successfully accomplished), by granting those who directly
suffer from them some everyday reward in recreation, but
rather of its profoundly transforming our society. To do this it
seeks to export its methods into every sector of activity, and
above all to promote the belief that all aspects of daily life can
also provide an element of entertainment. Laughter is the best
means of fostering consumption, the euphoria it induces being
bound to make consumers feel secure while at the same time
exonerating their hours of toil by giving them the double
reward of the product at the best price and the pleasure of
buying it. In fact it is no longer just different cultural attitudes
that are influenced by Las Vegas, but equally every area of civilization: technical know-how, the city, social organization, etc.
Las Vegas achieves the marvel of building a city, not to say a
way of life, on pure entertainment. Thus it succeeds in tipping
out the whole of civilization into the play pool where the
distinct forms of culture and technical know-how are ground
down and mixed up into a phosphorescent liquid. This means
that entertainment becomes a means of production like any
other, one which is already in operation in the start-ups and
other consultancies where, according to the claims of their
promoters, working should represent sheer enjoyment, a way
of playing with the social and economic rules.

In a world where the politics of entertainment decrees its
technological law in all aspects, however trivial, of the human
environment, distraction consequently loses its meaning of
diversion. It is no longer rest or relaxation. Entertainment thus
apparently allows itself to drift away from reality by appealing
to make-believe (which, in Las Vegas, assumes the appearance
of reference to fairy-tales, utopian places and a kind of mythi-
fied history) all the better to return to it, to stop it in its tracks
and force it to submit to its lapidary laws. This is an entertainment that invades reality rather than escaping from it. By

means of assorted trickery, entertainment colonizes the real in all its forms. It enjoins it to submit to the categorical imperatives of fun, under pain of being exiled as a figure of humdrum banality. As a result, in Las Vegas the interference of the playful with the social is integral. Like no other, the city that never sleeps has exploded the bounded space of the amusement park, freed spectacle from the dark, enclosed hall of the cinema, and put television screens on the walls of the buildings.

One can however ask oneself what possibilities remain for opposing this reality if its very distancing from leisure is thereby actually abolished. Once the boundary between the serious and the playful is effectively destroyed, what critical forms can there be to restore spaces of differentiation or moments of separation within the very heart of the civilization of total leisure? Over past centuries, entertainment, in its double form of compensation and contestation, always defined itself in contrast to a social reality that it was either forgetting or confronting. In the capital of Nevada, the phenomenon of fun has put an end to any counter possibility, unless it be the tragic one of the tedium and solitude that awaits anyone who refuses to join in the game.

Las Vegas is essentially a Pascalian city, but it is a Pascal without God, and without the wager, who would see no other choice for the creature truly abandoned by the divinity but that between boredom and entertainment, the inner void and the void outside, the infinitesimal nature of anguished awareness and the cosmic greatness of the world that takes your mind off things. In the face of this invasion of the everyday sphere by the system of alternative and absolute values, our way of feeling and acting finds itself constrained by a no less radical choice: either to adopt forthwith this binary way of life or to leave the city immediately. In its social and political excess, which in Las Vegas is expressed with a crystalline purity, entertainment has given up any distinction between fiction and reality, has fused everything into the single universe of glitz, and has turned back

116

against that everyday life which gave it refuge, in order to enslave it. So, if escapism still wishes to safeguard its engagement with the imagination, it must itself turn against entertainment. But how are we to counter diversion when it has thus become so universal? Or rather how are we to free ourselves from the overall grip of these tight-locked imaginary worlds which subjugate our reality rather than enriching it? A single possibility arises: fleeing from the city, without lingering or turning back, rediscovering the common sense of ordinary gestures and everyday speech, which, better than any critique, consolidate our close affinity with the natural and human environment. Leaving Las Vegas – that sums up the only way of salvation.

Vegas Vicky

With metronomic regularity, the steel and neon woman, a cowgirl encased in her phosphorescent bustier, lifts her electric leg every 30 seconds. Using her glitter-ringed eyes, she entices onlookers who peer under her skirts to see if any coins are lurking there that might give them a chance to recoup their losses. Tall as a five-storey Paris building, this female colossus of robotic eroticism winks at the whole town, a celestial and mechanical whore who as evening falls bedecks herself with gaudily-coloured halos and heats up the desert all by herself with her loose-woman ways.

Faithfully, the Sphinx of Fremont Street oversees the road into downtown. But make no mistake: her alluring looks mask a boundless cruelty. She is surrounded by screens on which astronomical sums flicker past, and her riddle consists in sequences of incomprehensible figures that she debits assiduously. Is that the amount she is asking for? The amount she is giving? Everyone has their doubts. When a client finally dares to challenge her, she casts a look full of lust and says her digital rosary unperturbed. But no one yet has been able to pay her price.

References

1   By using the etymologically incorrect term *zeropolis*, I
    deliberately set out to emphasize the inanity of repeated
    attempts by town planners, sociologists and philosophers
    to define the contemporary city in antiquated terms that
    variously christen it as *megalopolis, exopolis, metapolis, post-
    metropolis, peripolis*, etc, and also to locate the very essence
    of the urbanity of the future being developed in Las Vegas:
    in nothingness as a number.

2   Nick Tosches, 'Holy City', preface to *Literary Las Vegas*, ed.
    Mike Tronnes (Edinburgh, 1995), p. 15. For Tosches, the
    sanctity of the Mecca of gambling is probably connected
    with its duly inhuman talent for raising mediocrity to the
    heights of a ritual no less solemn and monumental than
    the rituals that have made the great monotheistic religions
    popular. It is this *passion* – in an almost Christlike sense of
    the word, by virtue of the public exposure to mockery and
    suffering, villainy and deceit — that forms the spirit of the
    city.

3   Thomas K. Wolfe, 'Las Vegas (What?), Las Vegas (Can't
    hear you! Too noisy), Las Vegas!!!!', in *Esquire* (February
    1964).

4   Mike Davis, *City of Quartz: Excavating the Future in Los
    Angeles* (London and New York, 1990), p. 244.

5   When we talk about Las Vegas as a utopia, this is not just a
    matter of analogy. The Nevada capital possesses the true
    characteristics of one. The most fundamental of these is
    probably the question of its geographical location. In the
    classic structure of the Utopia (found in More, Campanella

and Cabet), it is of cardinal importance that the ideal city should be situated well away from any other city, physically or temporally separated from the present civilisation by which it is going to be discovered, this frequently by accident. The Mojave Desert surrounding Las Vegas favours this spatial isolation which lends itself to separation from reality. Its 'geographical implausibility' (as Joan Didion puts it in 'Marrying Absurd', in *Literary Las Vegas*, op.cit., p. 163) consolidates the idea that what takes place there has absolutely no link with reality. So even before Las Vegas puts its fantasy decor and its ethos of immediate gratification on display, its setting alone is enough to make it a Utopia (*a non-place*).

6   Nick Tosches, 'Holy City', p. 15.

7   Hunter S. Thompson, 'Fear and Loathing in Las Vegas', in *Literary Las Vegas*, p. 149.

8   Frances Anderton and John Chase, *Las Vegas, The Success of Excess* (Cologne, 1997), p 37.

9   Robert Venturi, Denise Scott Brown and Steven Izenour, *Learning from Las Vegas* (Cambridge, MA, 1977).

10   Nathanael West, *Miss Lonelyhearts & The Day of the Locust* (New York, 1969), p. 61.

11   Jonathan Raban, *Hunting Mister Heartbreak* (London, 1990), p. 88.

12   Alan Hess, *Viva Las Vegas, After Hours Architecture* (San Francisco, 1993), p. 8.

13   Hess, *Viva Las Vegas*, p. 116.

14   Hess, *Viva Las Vegas*, p. 123.

15 Hess, *Viva Las Vegas*, p. 121.

16 Michael Ventura, 'Las Vegas: The Odds on Anything', in *Literary Las Vegas*, p. 167.

17 Ventura, 'Las Vegas: The Odds on Anything', p. 170: 'Another way to say this is that what Mormon pioneers, the Mafia, *and* the atomic military have in common is a keen, highly developed sense of Anything – a sense of Anything that felt a kinship to the place itself, as though this desert were calling to them.'

List of Photographs